My Life and Quest

BY
ARTHUR OSBORNE

SRI RAMANASRAMAM
Tiruvannamalai
2001

*Arunachala Ashrama
66-12 Clyde Street
Rego Park, New York 11374
(718) 575-3215*

© Sri Ramanasramam
Tiruvannamalai
First Edition, Year 2001
2000 Copies

ISBN No: 81-88225-20-7

Price: Rs. 60/-
CC No: 1061

Published by
V.S. Ramanan
President, Board of Trustees
Sri Ramanasramam
Tiruvannamalai 606 603
Tamil Nadu
INDIA
Tel: 91-4175-37292
Fax: 91-4175-37491
Email: alagamma@vsnl.com
Website: www.ramana-maharshi.org

Ink Sketch of Arunachala by Sri Ramana Maharshi

Designed and typeset at
Sri Ramanasramam
Printed by
Kartik Printers
Chennai 600 015

Publisher's Note

ARTHUR OSBORNE, one of the most ardent and well known of the devotees of Sri Bhagavan, was the founder-editor of *The Mountain Path*, the spiritual journal published by the Ashram. He is well known as the Editor of *Collected Works of Ramana Maharshi* and the author of *Ramana Maharshi and the Path of Self-Knowledge* and other works.

We are happy to bring out this autobiographical account of Arthur Osborne which should be of immense value to serious seekers since it carries a wealth of information on the spiritual path. The author's portrayal of the spiritual ministry of Sri Bhagavan is particularly moving.

We are thankful to Katya Douglas, the author's daughter for her kindness in giving the manuscript to us and permitting us to bring it out as an Ashram publication.

31st December 2001   PUBLISHER
Bhagavan's 122nd Jayanti   Sri Ramanasramam

Bhagavan Sri Ramana Maharshi
1879 — 1950

FOREWORD

MANY YEARS after my father's death in 1970, I opened an old suitcase and found several of his unpublished manuscripts. It is strange that they remained buried and unknown for so long, but perhaps now is the time for this story to be told. Reading through them it was intriguing to see how true his voice was, and how it endured over the years. One of these documents was his autobiography that he had entitled "The Mountain Path, My Quest".

Later when he founded the quarterly magazine for Ramanasramam he used the title "Mountain Path" for that, so we decided to leave it out of this work in order to avoid confusion.

It is an apt title for the chronicle of his life which was dedicated firstly, to finding the path, and once he was sure that he had found the right one he was utterly committed to it. His poetry as much as his prose show what a struggle it was for him at times, how he fought with darkness and despair, but, as he points out, a man who is climbing Mount Everest does not stop to play the violin. Through all his vicissitudes his faith in Bhagavan was unwavering, and Bhagavan recognised in him his humility and dedication. Sometimes when he was sitting in the hall with his eyes closed in meditation Bhagavan would look at him with such love that it could move one to tears. Even as a child I recognised this as something very special.

He was a very special person and father, but as he was the only one I had ever known I perhaps did not quite realise his uniqueness until much later. Of course some things were outstanding even to me. He writes about being quite gregarious as a young man; be that as it may, by the time he was an older man, and my father, he had become quite the opposite. He would talk, but he never chattered. I could ask him about anything that I wanted to know and get a concise answer, but he never talked randomly or just to fill a silence. He was a man of silence and he wore it like a cloak.

A couple of stories I remember sharply illustrate this quality in him.

Two men once came all the way from Delhi to Tiruvannamalai especially to meet him, and my mother seated them all on the veranda while she carried on with her work. After about an hour, hearing no sound from outside she assumed the men had left and came out. She was startled to see the three of them still sitting together in silence and she hastened to make conversation. They wanted to ask him many questions but were nervous or shy of initiating a discussion. When they eventually did leave my mother asked him why he hadn't spoken to them, why in fact he had left them sitting in silence for so long. He had no idea why she was upset. He said that he thought they wanted to be quiet but that if they had anything to talk to him about they only had to say so!

Some time after I had left home and was living with my husband in Pakistan, I came back on a visit. I had bought some old coins in the bazaar in Peshawar and I showed them to him, explaining that I had been told they were from the reign of some ancient king. He looked at them and said that one of the coins was certainly of a much later date than I supposed.

"How do you know?" I asked him. "I didn't think you were interested in old coins."

"I'm not," he told me, "but the date is written on the coin."

"It is written in Arabic!" I exclaimed. "I didn't know you could read Arabic. Why didn't you ever tell me?"

"Well, you never asked me," was his reply. He had in fact learned the language many years before but had not used it for vii

a long time. In all those years it had never occurred to him to mention that he spoke yet another language apart from Polish and French, and for all I know several more that I hadn't asked him about! As I said, he was not a man of many words, but those that he did speak were worth listening to.

My mother was also deeply devoted to Bhagavan although hers was more an intuitive devotion: her instinct was sure. When my father was interned in Bangkok at the beginning of the Second World War she had not one single word from him for two years, and then a telegram came from the War Ministry to say that he had been killed. At the time we were staying with our friends the Sharmas in Madras. Mrs. Sharma was terribly upset on my mother's behalf and tried to comfort her.

My mother was relatively calm. She kept saying, "Don't worry, it is a mistake. If Arthur were dead I would know it. I know he is not dead. It is a mistake."

Of course they all thought that she was unbalanced with grief, and Mrs. Sharma was so upset by this seemingly irrational behaviour that my mother ended up trying to comfort her, while she herself remained unwavering in her belief that her husband was alive, and sure enough a few days later there was another telegram saying in effect that they had got the wrong Osborne. Her intuition guided her, and her faith in Bhagavan who, when my little brother Adam asked him to keep his daddy safe, had assented. This, and her own instinct gave her the knowledge and the fortitude to sense the truth and to recognise the mistake for what it was. Later we got all his letters simultaneously, and apparently he also only heard from us after two years.

As the oldest of the three of us and the only one who could write or who, in fact remembered my father, I was allowed to send my own letters although there was a rule that each one should be no longer than twenty-five words. I spent a lot of time trying very hard to fit all that I had to say into that allocation and I would save up the things I wanted to tell him and practise distilling them into very few words; this did not seem as difficult then as it does in retrospect, as children seem to be born with the ability to accept whatever life offers and to take it for granted. We lose this talent as we grow up and then have to work hard to reclaim it. Now I feel how very distressing it must have been for both my parents to keep going in the face of such a long silence. Luckily they had Bhagavan.

The years after he came home from the war were, for us children, a great joy. Our almost mythical daddy was back with us and we revelled in it. He brought a new perspective into our lives. My mother had struggled alone throughout the war with three very small children and an uncertain future. She was, for us, the sole authority and it was sometimes difficult for her to cope with our constant ability to get up to mischief. With the arrival of my father our horizons broadened. We loved his wisdom and his innate sense of justice. We loved his subtle sense of humour and the way he would tease our mother with an absolutely straight face until we all burst out laughing. . . her too. Looking back I sense that the pleasure my parents felt at the end of their long separation brought laughter into our lives.

My father was an enthusiastic gardener and I enjoyed walking round with him in the mornings as he observed all the growing things and tended to them. He knew by instinct what each plant needed and he inculcated in me a love of gardens that I have never lost.

We would sometimes sit outside at night and he pointed out the various stars and constellations. He also told me stories from mythology that fascinated me as much as they had enthralled him as a child. When we were little he told us the most wonderful bedtime tales; there was the ongoing saga of a pixy that lived in a magnolia flower and travelled on moonbeams. Astonishing though it might seem, the three of us began to look forward to bedtime! He was a natural storyteller.

Many years later when I came home for a long visit with my little daughter Aruna we were concerned about her missing too much schooling, so my father undertook to teach her English and history. They sat outside on the veranda, his deep voice telling her stories and her childish treble interjecting an occasional question. He made it all so interesting that I sat myself in the doorway inside, out of sight, in order to listen. My mother was sitting in the same position in the other room. She caught my eye and smiled, and then she put her finger to her lips and we were joined in a conspiracy of silence.

At the time when my parents were seeking for a spiritual path it was not at all a popular point of view. Nowadays, in spite of, or perhaps because of, the dangerous and materialistic world we live in, more and more people are interested in finding a deeper truth. Inadequate gurus or bogus sects unfortunately lead many astray. Bhagavan said often that we are not the body. His teaching is as valid and alive today as it was when he sat in the hall wearing a body for all to see.

For my father, his coming to Tiruvannamalai was an affirmation of his Quest and having confirmed that Bhagavan was his guru, he never looked back.

After retiring from his work in Calcutta he founded and edited *The Mountain Path* until his health gave out. Knowing he couldn't continue he prepared and left in perfect order ten editorials which were for whoever was to follow him. As it happens my mother took on this task for a time, which was especially difficult for her as English was not her mother tongue. She did it out of love and loyalty until her health too gave out. Their relationship, a union of opposites, was crucial to both their lives and my father's last words were to her. He said "Thank you". Then he died as he had lived, without fuss, and he is buried in the garden he created and loved.

He was only sixty-four.

The war years had taken their toll of him and also the intensity of his inner quest placed an enormous strain on his body because he made no compromise.

The precious legacy he left us is in his writing. We can travel with him along the road and experience how he dealt with the problems that beset all of us. Reading again of his inner life and struggle I am heartened that an ordinary human being could find in himself such steadfastness and such ability to remain resolute in the face of all obstacles. It is surely an example to anyone on the mountain path.

31st December 2001   KATYA DOUGLAS
Bhagavan's 122nd Jayanti   Tiruvannamalai

Arthur Osborne and his wife Lucia
in their garden at Tiruvannamalai

Osborne's children on Arunachala.
(l to r): Adam, Frania and Catherine

CONTENTS

Chapter		page
	Publisher's Note	iii
	Foreword	v
1	Beginnings	1
2	A Station Passed Through	4
3	Change of Course	8
4	Oxford Rejected	12
5	Down to the Nadir	22
6	Marriage	26
7	The Quest Begins	29
8	Adventures on the Path	45
9	Tribulation	69
10	Bhagavan Sri Ramana Maharshi	89
11	I Become a Writer — and Cease to Be One	115
12	Brief Eternity	134
13	Retirement	143
14	Continued Quest	152
Addendum	POEMS	
	A Testament	171
	The Guru	183
	To Arunachala	184
	To Bhagavan	186
	Brief Eternity	189
	The Tiger	190
	The Indewller-II	190

xii

POEMS *(contd)* page

The Initiatic Death	191
The Dark Night	192
Desolation	193
The Lady of Shalott	194
Complete Your Work!	195
The Sleeping Beauty	196
Anatta	197
The Two Windows	198
To Whom?	199
The World	200
The World-II	201
The Shakti	202
Ergo Non Sum	202
The Dream-Self	203
Others-II	204
The Expanse	205
Fantastic Things	206
To Christians	207
What Remains?	208
The Song	209
This Dream	210
The Poet	211
Day and Night	212
The Waning Moon	213
The Elixir of Youth	214
Otherness	215
The Wind	217

1

Beginnings

As a small boy there were three books that I read over and over again *The Knights of King Arthur, Asgard and the Gods* and *The Arabian Nights*. It was King Arthur that was my favourite. My mother had a leather bound edition that she had acquired as a school prize, and there was not a page of it without my grubby finger marks. Next in preference came the Norse legends. The more sophisticated mythology of Greece never appealed to me, but there was a wild grandeur about that of the Norseman that stirred me so deeply that it has remained in my memory ever since — the arrogant immensity of the giants in the time of their ascendancy, so that even a blow of Thor's hammer was felt no more than an acorn falling on the brow. And then the return of Thor to power. How the giants had stolen his hammer Mjolnir and hidden it deep within the earth and would only return it at the price of Odin's daughter as bride to one of them; how the gods tricked them, dressing Thor up in brides clothes and sending him veiled to their palace.

Even through the veil the flash of his eyes could be seen. Then the story grew tense as the bridegroom asked for the veil to be removed but the pretended bride insisted that Mjolnir should be first placed in her lap. Then, when this was done, how Thor laughed aloud and tore off the veil as he rose to his feet, brandishing Mjolnir, and how he left their whole palace in smoking ruins. This and the more tragic stories: the killing of Baldur the Beautiful, the treachery of Loki, the rise of his fearsome sons from the underworld, and the end of everything in the last terrible battle of Ragnarok. As I grew older I began vaguely to feel the mystery of symbolism behind the stories. Indeed it is remarkable all three books should have been allegories of the universal doctrines of the quest. Not only did I read these stories, but I constantly made up my own, especially about King Arthur and his knights, telling them to myself while walking or doing things. This was my secret. I never told any one about it. Unknowingly, I must have been telling the stories in verse, because I remember puzzling why it was that if I added one word, that is one syllable, the sentence sounded wrong, while if I added two it sounded right again.

The time came when I began to consider these imaginings as sin and resolved to stop them, but try as I would I always slipped back into them. Once, as a penance and a constant reminder, I decided to wear a knotted cord around my loins, as I had read of medieval monks doing. So I found an old piece of garden rope, made knots in it, and tied it tightly round my waist. However, this gave me stomach ache and I could not think of any other way of tying that would hold up, so I abandoned the idea.

A favourite daydream at this time was of some mighty king in a far off land in time and space. Many people came to him, bringing all imaginable wealth and pleasures; and then I would come in a monk's robe offering him renunciation and hardship. I was to discover later that the king was the ego enthroned amid the pleasures of this world and then bidden to renounce and set forth on the lonely quest.

All this does not mean that I was a morose or gloomy child. On the contrary, I was exuberant, as a Sagittarian should be, fun-loving, delighted when visitors came or when we went out anywhere. Only there was this inner current of life also, and it was something I did not speak about.

Extrovert or introvert? I do not believe the definitions are anywhere near so widely applicable as commonly supposed: a person of high vitality is often both, a person of low vitality neither. Certainly I was both to a high degree.

2

A Station Passed Through

THE NEXT POWERFUL influence on my life was the Yorkshire Moors. Perhaps it could be described as a vision of beauty — the long sweep of the hills, the heather glowing purple in the distance and springy underfoot, the profusion of wild flowers — marsh orchids, and many others — the wild strawberries growing by the roadside and, above all, the sombre pine-woods with the wind moaning through them. And yet I had known beautiful country before and have known it since, and never had it such power over me. I loved it in rain and mist as well as in sunshine. It became connected in my mind with the Norse legends and the vital power of the Northlands. It seemed something too sacred to speak about, and I never did speak about it.

The last time we spent our summer holidays there I must have been about fifteen. The spell was as strong as ever. It was then that I wrote my first sonnet. I was sitting alone on a hillside and took out a new notebook that I happened to have in my breast pocket and wrote a sonnet about the moors on the first page. I decided to write one on each page and give it to my mother for a birthday present when it was full. I don't know whether I ever wrote another poem in it; I certainly never gave it to any one. In the same holiday I wrote a lyric on the moors and the pine trees that I long regarded as a great poem. Juvenile as it was, it was written with genuine inspiration. I have long since forgotten it.

The same holiday we made friends with a local farmer, whom I will call Bob Thorpe, an uncouth looking fellow, unshaven, with a broad North Riding accent, and yet a great lover of beauty and a reader of poetry. When he sat on a hillside beside me, reciting Tennyson and Milton, there was much less of an accent in his speech. He too loved the moorlands. Instead of a compact farm in the valley around his farmhouse he had his fields scattered on the various hills because he loved walking from hill to hill. There were those who said that it was also because it gave him an excuse for walking over the squire's grounds and that he left a trail of rabbit snares as he went; in fact, poaching was as much a business with him as farming.

I never liked games, neither cricket and football nor the lighter games such as tennis and badminton. I played as much as was inescapable at school and no more. On the other hand I loved gardening. We had an orchard behind the house and a garden for growing flowers and vegetables, and my father and I did all the work of it. Whether it was the heavy work of digging and manuring or sowing seeds, pruning fruit trees, even weeding, I loved the very contact with the earth and the growing things. When, therefore, harvest started and Bob Thorpe let me work for him as an unpaid labourer it was he who was doing me a favour. We worked from first daylight to dusk, taking time off at midday to rest in the shade and eat the cold meat that the

6 *My Life and Quest*

womenfolk brought to the field for us. It was an old-fashioned, simple reaper and we bound the sheaves by hand and arranged them in stooks. I had never spent so enjoyable a holiday.

Farming appealed to me and might have fulfilled my nature but my father had other plans for me and would not consider such a possibility.

When I say that this outcome, supposing it to have been possible, would have been the only fulfilment of my life, that does not mean that missing it was a cause for regret; indeed, it was a cause for rejoicing. The only real measure of success in life is the state of mind and character one has attained when the time comes to leave it. The only full success is spiritual enlightenment, realization of the Self. The life in a man is returning ineluctably to its Source, to Oneness with the Self, like a river to the ocean. This lifetime is an episode on the path, and all that matters is the distance from the goal when the episode ends. This depends on two things: first on the position from which this lifetime begins, that is to say the stage on the road already attained in past existences, whether human or not; secondly on the wisdom and determination with which one presses forward in this lifetime. There is no injustice in the different stages from which man begins life's course or in the different degrees of understanding and determination with which they are endowed, for that concerns only speed, and impatience is a purely human disease. The difference does not affect the universal order or the final outcome. Indeed, from the viewpoint of the universal order, the courses man follows can be compared rather to rivers flowing into the ocean than to men trudging the road on a pilgrimage — a lifetime representing not the whole course of the river but only a certain stretch of it. Even though some meander or stagnate or even turn backwards, while others flow swift and strong, all plunge finally into the same ocean. There is not even any question of earlier or later, since time does not come into it when the rivers' courses are viewed as a whole from the air. But for the individual time does make a difference. So long as he feels himself to be an individual the striving is real and it is the symbol of the pilgrim that applies, not that of the river. And for the pilgrim, wasted time is wasted opportunity. A whole lifetime, a whole day's journey on the pilgrimage, may be wasted, idling by the roadside, wandering a field, or even going back; and then the next day's journey will be more arduous and its starting point less advantageous.

It is true that by no means all envisage life as a purposeful journey. Happy are those who do and who act on the knowledge; but even those who do not are advancing or regressing according to whether they weaken or strengthen the grip of the ego, cutting some of its tentacles or putting out new ones. Fundamentally, the weakening and final dissolution of the ego is the purpose of all religions; and it is religion which is the most efficacious for accomplishing this task, although selfless service of others, and even of animals and plants, can also be effective to some extent. Whatever weakens the ego is good, whatever strengthens it bad. Thus, it may be advantageous for a person to be uprooted rather than to strike root. Certainly it was for me. If destiny had closed the circle, leading me to contentment on a Yorkshire farm, the journey might have ended there and this lifetime been wasted. As it happened, this episode was like a station that the train stops at long enough to look out of the window and then travels on.

3

Change of Course

I NEVER WENT back to the moors. Life now took a new course. The beacon ahead to which I steered was an Oxford scholarship. I have the methodical tenacity in pursuing a goal which one would expect of a moon in Capricorn. At present the goal was an idealized Oxford; later it was to be the supreme goal of Nirvana. Between the two intervened a period with no envisaged goal, when I tossed adrift on a stormy sea. At present Oxford seemed like an alabaster city of dreams in the mists ahead and I aimed steadily at getting there. Not only was it the gateway to a good career but, in itself, a haven of culture from the bleak money-cult of the West Riding. In fact, refusal to accept a materialist world was already working in my mind and, the true alternative having not yet been descried, an idealized Oxford served as an imaginary substitute for it.

My school trained boys in classics, science and mathematics, but an enthusiastic history master captured my interest and got the headmaster's permission to coach me for a history scholarship. That was before the day of the welfare state, when a country grant came automatically to all who obtained entrance to a university. For me it was a scholarship or nothing.

Side by side with persistent study I found time for other reading also — philosophical writers like Ruskin and Carlyle, though not pure philosophy; theology as well, such as the works of Dean Inge who was then in vogue; also much poetry. My special delight was when I was left alone in the house and was able to read poetry aloud. I also enjoyed whatever humour came my way — Pickwick, the plays of W.S. Gilbert, the Ingoldsby Legends. Except for an occasional humorous novel, I read no fiction. It seemed a waste of time with so much knowledge to acquire and philosophy to ponder. Although little enough spending money came my way, I began to accumulate a small library.

I thought of myself as a future writer. Looking round at the sunset sky from a windy hill one evening, the conviction came to me with an intensity of a revelation: "I could write poems if there were anything important enough to write about". Several times in the course of my life I recalled this, saying: "Surely what I feel now is important enough?" But it never was.

On another occasion, walking across the fields into town, I had a strange dream that I should some day write a book that would begin in prose and then, attaining too high a vibration for prose, continue in poetry, and finally transcend speech altogether, ending in silence.

There were no buses on the roads in those days, and it was a two-mile walk to school in the morning and back in the evening; often four times a day when I came home for lunch. I must have been about sixteen when, as I was walking home one day, a vivid and intense feeling of the reality of death came over me — why should I accumulate a library, why should I accumulate

10   *My Life and Quest*

anything at all, when death was inevitable? There was nothing sad or tragic about the thought and no fear; it was not a feeling of despondency or revolt, but simply of the inevitability of death. It passed and effected no permanent change, but at least it left an impression too vivid to fade. It was at the same age that an experience of death overwhelmed Ramana, who was to become the Maharshi, and destroyed his ego once and for all, leaving him thenceforth established immutably in the Self (see my *Ramana Maharshi and the Path of Self-Knowledge*, page 18-19, Rider & Co). It is very seldom that the path can thus be completed in a single step, only in those rare cases where obstacles have already been overcome in a previous life, leaving the ultimate attainment within grasp. More often it is a path of striving for a lifetime, seldom indeed brought to a conclusion before life ends. However, it may be natural for the first intuition of it to occur at this age, when the mind is already fully active and worldly unwisdom has not yet closed over it like a dense cloud, hiding the face of Reality.

Religion already meant a lot to me. At this time I came under the influence of a Welsh clergyman called Morgan, a spare but powerfully built man dominating and combative, utterly dedicated and tense with nervous energy. That he was a boxing blue and an authority on rugby football impressed me not at all, that he was a keen wit very much. He ran into opposition through introducing beauty into his church and its services. Typical of him was that he painted the pews bright green instead of the usual dull brown, saying that he wanted to wake people up when they came into the church, not put them to sleep. To give us courage he introduced street processions and small prayer meetings conducted by laymen, and I took part in both. I had read *Gitanjali* and its sequel, Tagore's books of prose poems, and was fascinated by them as the nearest thing to mystical knowledge I had yet found (though how far distant from it I was later to understand) and — foreshadowing of things to come — at one such prayer meeting that I conducted I read out a poem by Tagore and explained that, although not a Christian, he had the same faith and understanding. Those present expressed agreement.

The second strong influence on me at that time was Mr. Lance, my history master. He was a loyal son of Christ Church and eager that I should go there too. However, the Oxford colleges were divided into three groups for scholarship purposes, and in my year the Christ Church group came last of the three. It would be obviously too reckless to wait for that, so he suggested my going up to try for a scholarship a year early. The headmaster agreed that it would be useful for me to have the experience, not that there was any chance of my getting in. It was, however, pointed out to me that it was unwise for a boy from a grammar school like ours to put Christ Church first on his list of preferences; he would not be chosen anyway, and it would make the colleges he had put lower down on the list less likely to accept him. However, I stuck to my guns, or rather to Mr. Lance's guns. In the autumn of 1924 I went up to Oxford as a scholar of Christ Church, just turned eighteen, a year before my time.

4

OXFORD REJECTED

MY TUTORS LET me know that they were grooming me for a fellowship of All Souls and a career as an Oxford don. For two years I went along with them, and then in the third year almost stopped work, cut myself off from college and the university life and in general made myself unacceptable. I was conceited enough to think that I could easily make a living by writing whether I had a profession or not. I was becoming profoundly disillusioned with Oxford and more and more incompatible. I had therefore no goal at which to aim. That of going to Oxford had been achieved; that now proposed, of an academic career, failed to appeal; and the true goal of life had not yet been revealed.

I had expected more of Oxford than it could give: a home of culture where men were interested in all that could not be bought for money. I threw myself into the new life with enthusiasm. I was assiduous in attending lectures, studying in libraries and in my room, composing essays for my bi-weekly tutorials. I also plunged eagerly into the new social life. Scarcely a day passed without my being invited out or inviting others to my rooms. However, before even the first term ended, there was a chill feeling of disillusionment. Where I had expected understanding I found triviality. Gradually I withdrew upon myself until, by the end of my third year, there were not half a dozen people in the whole university whom I knew well enough to drop in on uninvited. I shrank back from Oxford life: never spoke in the Union, though fond of debating; never acted in the OUDS, though attracted to the stage; never wrote for the *Isis* or *Cherwell*, whichever it was called — the university weekly — although I considered myself a writer.

The inner rejection extended to studies as well as people. History had held my interest at school partly as the pageant of great men and events and partly as a study of long-term developments; but when it was offered to me in the guise of research work — spending months deciphering the rent rolls of a 12th century village in order to write a thesis on the economic basis of medieval land tenure, ferreting out all the references to a tenth-rate Tudor politician whom I should not be interested to meet if he lived today — and when this was proposed to me as an occupation in life, I shrank back from it. Twice in future years I was to find that when I saw a field of knowledge to possess intrinsic value I could read voraciously and study meticulously, but not just research for it's own sake, not amassing details about some question that I felt to be unimportant and in which I was uninterested.

I quite realized, of course, that history or any other discipline of modern learning — sociology, astronomy, marine biology, whatever it may be — advances through the endless, patient, often anonymous research of scholars working either in battalions or deployed singly to strategic points, much of their work infructuous but some of it producing results which can modify a whole theory or inaugurate a hypothesis. To doubt the importance of such research would be to reject the very basis of modern civilization. I do not reject it. That does not mean that I advocate wearing handloom cloth or working by candlelight or any such puerilities. So long as one lives in the modern world it is senseless not to conform to its outer conditions; what is to be rejected is its sense of values, its conviction of its own superiority and belief in the intrinsic worth of the sciences on which it is based, in fact its whole *Weltanschauung*. If the rejection of that were sufficiently widespread it would lead to rejection of its outer forms also, but that is not likely to happen easily or peacefully.

In the social order based on a real respect for human nature (which includes appreciation of man's spiritual potentialities) a man's work for the community involves his inner development also. If he is a craftsman making furniture or building houses, his work is an art and he takes pride in its completion; it is also based on a symbolism reflecting his own self-building; if he is a student, his studies tend to the development of his understanding and burgeoning of his character, rectifying warped or stunted tendencies in him. But the modern mechanical civilization uses men as instruments whether they be labourers or scholars. Just as a workman tends to his machines with no consideration for his own development, so a scholar contributes his fragment of research totally alien to wisdom or self-knowledge. It is not true that society is greater than a man, nor is it expedient that one man should die for the good of the people. An anthill is greater than the single ants that compose it, but man has a divinity in his nature which potentially contains and transcends this whole world; and a society which denies this by treating men as instruments, providing no means for their spiritual development, is eating out its own vitals, leaving itself an empty shell. Traditionally it has always been held that the search for Truth or Knowledge is sacred and requires no motive or justification, that is, a fit end to which to devote one's life. That is true, but it refers to knowledge of direct or indirect spiritual import, knowledge which gradually illumines or transforms the seeker; to speak in the same terms of the accumulation of mere factual knowledge is a parody; and that is what is done.

I did not know all this at the time, but I intuitively rejected research as a sterile use to which to put one's years of life. I intuitively rejected modern civilization — not indeed with any knowledge of its sickness, not knowing that my antipathy to it was more than poetic and romantic, but with a deep feeling of its inadequacy. I did not know what I wanted of Oxford, but I felt bitterly that I had not found it.

To some extent I knew. I knew that I wanted spiritual guidance. The answer to that would be that it is not Oxford's purpose to supply this. That is true, but a deeper counter-current would be that a country or civilization whose highest centre of learning and culture is indifferent to spiritual values, neither inculcating nor denying them, simply ignoring them, is in a very bad way.

Here were young men receiving the best education their country had to offer, some of them studying its language and literature, others its history, and all in utter ignorance of its majestic traditions, of the intrepid strivings of its mystics, the paths to Beatitude that they had trod and the final supreme achievement, the Mystic Union. Ignorant not merely of their actual testimony but of their very existence, not even knowing that there was a goal to life, that there were paths leading to it,

16 *My Life and Quest*

and that men had trod these paths and left records of their ascent. One of my friends took Sanskrit for his degree, and he also, during his years of study, was never let into the secret that there is anything of spiritual interest in Sanskrit literature.

It is remarkable how all doors to spiritual growth were closed to me at this time — or opened only to reveal a bleak, cheerless interior. At first I joined one or two others from my college in going to weekly evangelical meetings in town.

We sat on upright chairs in a bare room while impromptu prayers were said, and some one gave a talk on being saved and what a wonderful experience it was. Well, I thought, it must be a wonderful experience for him, but I don't seem to have it. So I stopped going. During most of my first year I attended morning chapel instead of roll call — twenty minutes instead of two. I was usually the only person there. I also went to some special kind of evening service that was held in the chapel once or twice a week. But it seemed cold and lifeless and meant nothing to me and I gradually stopped going. Neither the college chaplain nor any other ecclesiastic (and there were some, because Christ Church chapel is also Oxford Cathedral) offered any help or encouragement or even seemed aware of my seeking. During one vacation I went to stay at the Christ Church mission in East London. It was doing useful social work but there was nothing spiritual about it. I visited an Anglo-Catholic priory but felt no atmosphere such as might impel me to probe deeper. I toyed with the idea of Catholicism, but more for its poetic than its religious appeal. I made friends with the two Indian undergraduates at my college — one a Hindu and the other a Muslim — and became a frequent visitor at the Majlis, the Indian undergraduates' club, with the vague hope, based on recollections of Tagore, that it would lead to some spiritual contact, but

Arthur Osborne 17

nothing of the sort transpired. Most Indians abroad either reject their spiritual heritage or are reticent about it, fearful of not being considered modern. I joined a mystic society which was to have weekly meetings with talks on various branches of mysticism. The first meeting was held at Balliol in the rooms of Antony Mathew, one of the few friends I had at Oxford, a delightful person, heavy in build, light and graceful in manner, sociable and aloof at the same time. Some wealthy members of the club had brought a gong with a deep, mellow tone to announce the beginning of the meeting. Antony provided mulled claret and Turkish and Egyptian cigarettes. The gong was struck and the talk started. A South African scholar, a few years older than the rest of us and said to be immensely learned in such matters, was giving a talk on the Buddha. It was entirely made up of trivialities and contained nothing whatever of spiritual interest. And that was the end. The club never met again because it turned out that none of us knew anything to talk about. I never heard what happened to the gong. In distress I wrote to Morgan to ask him what he had done about spiritual thinking when he was at Oxford, and he wrote back that he hadn't done any. A chill came over me as I read that. It seemed a betrayal. Even Rosamond offered no help in this direction. I wrote to her that I was determined to understand Christ's miracles and she ignored that part of my letter in her reply. Perhaps, as a devout Catholic, she felt that faith was enough and that it was sacrilegious to want to understand.

Rosamond was a serene and gracious person, reminiscent of green lawns and summer flowers, far from the sombre pinewoods of the North. Scholarly, interested in art and poetry, she was at the same time normal and sensible — all that I was not. We were old friends as soon as we met. I felt that I had

18   *My Life and Quest*

known her always. Yet I never thought of asking her to marry me. Looking back, I can see that there were several occasions when my mind might at a touch have turned in that direction, but the touch was never given. In fact, all might-have-beens are an illusion; what did not happen never really lay within the bounds of possibility. Rosamond's conviction that I should become a great poet was bracing.

The frustration that I met with on every side in seeking spiritual guidance led me to turn the more enthusiastically to poetry. In my second year Denzil Batchelor came up and we immediately became close friends. He was a young man with shining brown eyes and a glowing voice, full of glory and tragedy. His energy was prodigious — poetry, football, drink, work, social life, and always tragically in love. I never doubted that he was one of the world's great poets; and this also made it easier for me to believe that I was another. I even followed suit in persuading myself that I was a tragic lover, choosing for the purpose an actress ten years my senior whom I had scarcely spoken to. Only many years later, going over such scraps of Denzil's poems as had stuck in my memory, did I realize that they were just melodious words, saying nothing. My own were not even that.

Even apart from personal ability there was the question of the spirit of the age, a force as impalpable but almost as binding as the law of averages. If you toss a coin it is equally likely to come down heads or tails; and if you toss it a hundred times this applies equally each single time. Therefore, in theory, it should be equally likely to come down heads all the hundred times. But in fact the law of averages is so rigorous that it will not vary more than two or three times either side of fifty. Similarly, it should theoretically be possible for a Tennyson to flourish in

Arthur Osborne 19

the age of Pope or a Pope in the age of Tennyson, but it does not happen so. Even when a writer seems to be out of touch with the spirit of the age or voluntarily hostile to it, he will usually be found to represent either an underground current of opposition or the rising tide of tomorrow beating on the crumbling cliffs of yesterday. In the twenties of this century, in the disillusionment following the First World War, cacophony was a desideratum of style and sophisticated superficiality of content. Neither Denzil nor I had the cast of mind or the approach to poetry that was then called modern. There were indeed two directions in which some living aspiration was being canalised, but neither of them affected us, or so far as I was aware, the Oxford of our time. One was Communism. It was the age when enthusiasts turned hopefully to Communism as a blueprint for a new utopia, only to be disillusioned later by the stark reality. The other was the spiritual revolt against materialist, mechanized modern civilization which was already flowing in many streams, for which I was searching half unwittingly and wholly in vain. After leaving Oxford I was isolated from the trend of things, at first of necessity and later from choice; and when, in the fifties, I was ready to write my books the streams had swollen to torrents; the development of myself had to some extent been reflected in the world, so that I found myself expressing the spirit of a new age and the books that I was then in a condition to write were such as the publishers were looking for. This does not mean, of course, that the world of today can be called spiritual — the very idea is ludicrous — but it does not mean that the anti-spiritual trend that set in with the Renaissance has run its course, terminating in the total denial of the age of Darwin, Marx and Freud, which Communism seeks to perpetuate, and that an opposite current is now flowing, back to a sense of spiritual reality. It is still a minority movement, as every Renaissance must be, but if these were normal times one might regard it as the wave of the future. However, they are not, and it may be that the world as we know it has no future, that this is the time of separation which Christ foretold long ago, between those who reject all wisdom and guidance, clinging only to the superficialities of life, and those who turn back with renewed energy in quest of meaning.

I had a contemporary at Christ Church who had real skill in writing verse and who was, moreover, in accord with the spirit of the age, and he therefore became famous as a poet. That was W.H. Auden. I knew him by sight but do not recollect ever speaking to him.

Writer or not, Oxford was not my destiny. It would have been as great a tragedy, as much the waste of a lifetime, if the circle had closed there as if it had closed earlier on a Yorkshire farm. It was an intuitive recognition that it would have been evading the fight of whose existence I did not yet know and accepting instead an easy establishment. However, I could not explain this to any one at the time because I did not know it myself.

To say that some one's destiny is not in a certain port does not absolve him from responsibility for the navigation. In spiritual things, statements which appear contradictory can both be true, expressing different aspects or levels of truth. For instance, Christ could say, from one standpoint, that evil must needs come, but he could immediately follow it up from another with a denunciation of those through whom it comes—which would be illogical and unjust if both statements were made from the same standpoint. Similarly, the *Quran* states that evil-doers can act as they do only by the divine will, and yet in another place it denounces them for putting forward this very plea in their own defence. The former viewpoint is cosmic and the latter individual, and each are valid on its own plane. (Actually, there is also a third standpoint, higher than either, the metaphysical; but from that the question of responsibility does not arise). To revert to a symbol used earlier in this book, the former is like viewing a landscape from the air, when the entire course of the river exists simultaneously in the eternal present, the timeless now; the latter is like a man in a boat, for whom the part of the river already navigated is past and that ahead is future. The course that lies ahead of him may be already marked on the map, but he has not access to the map and does not know what it is; also it is not drawn by any arbitrary whim but is due to the lie of the land, the force of the current and the obstacles interposed to its flow.

Had I possessed spiritual understanding at this time I could have remained at Oxford without betrayal, or sought a position elsewhere or simply left everything to take its course. As it was, my staying on would have been a betrayal but my making no other provision was an act not of faith but improvidence. It is the motive that makes an act right or wrong. Unfortunately a man can seldom mismanage his own life without hurting others also.

5

DOWN TO THE NADIR

THE LAST TERM ended and I packed up and left. I did not even trouble to attend the official degree-taking ceremony.

An immediate income became necessary; no use thinking any longer of future royalties on unwritten books. With some difficulty I obtained a post in a tenth-rate boarding school. The life was uncongenial, but even so it never occurred to me to regret not having stayed on at Oxford.

I was seriously considering becoming a Catholic in order to renounce the world and enter a monastery. Before taking up my teaching post I called at the Catholic church in my hometown to talk it over with the local priest. To my surprise I found this a flourishing institution with several incumbents. I was fortunate in contacting there Father Daly, an Irish Jesuit with an adventurous spirit, a simple, good-hearted man with whom I had more affinity than I should have had with some one of a more scholarly type. He was elderly then and retired to a more sedentary post owing to a weak heart, but most of his life he had spent in tropical Africa. He advised me that, if I made the decision, I should find the Benedictine order most suited to my temperament. I went for a number of doctrinal talks with him. The thing I found hardest to swallow was Adam's apple. I was told that I must believe that it was the sin of physical greed over a physical apple that caused the Fall. Even though I knew nothing yet of religious symbolism, I felt intuitively that this was a sterile parody of a profound truth. However, the scheme was not rejected for this or any other doctrinal reason but was gradually pushed aside during the months that followed by the zest for life in me — which means simply that the spiritual impetus was too weak, for when the real doorway opened several years later it called forth an aspiration against which no worldly zest could stand.

Within a year I had to give up my job on account of illness. When I recovered the Oxford University Appointments Board informed me of two possibilities — one at an Italian Archaeological College in Palestine, and the other as a private tutor in a Polish country family. I applied for both and both accepted me. The former was a chance to retrieve my position in an academic career; the latter was a dead end. However, the former refused to advance my passage money. They were willing to refund it when I arrived but I had not got it. I was no longer on good terms with my father, so instead of asking him for it straight out I asked his advice which job to take. He advised the Polish one. He was a practical, level-headed person, so I could only wonder what his motive was in advising what he must have known to be the wrong choice: whether it was because of the passage money or because the college was Catholic and knowing my leaning in that direction, he feared that I might be lost forever to a religion he abominated. Actually, if I had put the matter plainly to him, asking him outright to advance me the fare, I do not think he would have refused. There were also one or two other people who would probably have made the advance if I had asked them, but it never occurred to me to do so. I followed my destiny to Poland.

For nearly a year I lived in a Polish manorial house on a large estate, read little, wrote next to nothing, met few people, more or less stagnated.

At the end of that time I got a job helping with an evening school in the Upper Silesian mining and industrial town of Katowice. When I got there I found that it was not really an evening school at all; only a lecturer in English at Cracow University, a cautious, dapper little man, had started evening courses in English at Katowice, where he came by train two or three times a week to run them. The courses prospered. There was a boom in English owing to American industrial investment. He was glad to have an Englishman, and an Oxford graduate at that, to help him, but was too prudent to mention the fact in his advertisements — only his own name appeared. Next year, however, the beginnings of the postwar crisis began to be felt. The demand for English slumped and the courses could no longer support two.

Within three years of leaving Oxford I had come right down to the nadir — no job, no profession, no prospects, just making a living by giving private lessons to foreigners. Apart from the outer conditions, I was degenerating in myself also, tending to become superficial in life and cynical in outlook. The attempt to find an answer in religion had failed, and I no longer even went to church or read religious or philosophical books. The dream of being a professional writer had not materialised. I had wanted to write. Even the dream of a great love seemed to have eluded me and degenerated into a facile attraction to women. Nevertheless, some parts of the fortress still held — idealism and a sense of honour and great simplicity.

Actually, I had been shielded from the world during this time of decline when it would have been easy to lose grip— first in a boarding school, then a sick-bed, then a country house. Only now was I cast on to the waters of modern city life and in danger of dissipating my energies a hundred ways, with resultant weakening and superficiality. However, I had been a very short time in Katowice before my attention began to be concentrated on a lady of great charm and poise who came to the courses. She was tall and well built, with a pale complexion and dark, wavy hair. What first attracted me was an impression of great self-control and something secret about her eyes and smile betokening hidden wealth of personality. I was soon in love and decided that this was the wife for me. Such was my exuberance and folly that it did not even occur to me what a poor offer I was as a husband in view of the mess I had made of my life.

6

Marriage

MY MARRIAGE was the first wise thing I ever did. Even materially it marked the end of the descent and the beginning of the upward swing, for soon after it was agreed I received an offer of a post as English master at a government college for training ships' officers and engineers in the new port of Gdynia. They were looking for a suitable person and someone had mentioned my name.

It was quite a while before it was agreed upon, because the lady was not at first convinced. The perseverance and one-pointedness to convince her was a sort of rehearsal for the spiritual training to come later. Even at the time I felt it to be a process of strengthening like the forging of steel through fire. An indication of her nobility of character was that my lack of job or prospects was not one of the things that made her hesitate. She herself was working at the time as a secretary and translator to the general manager of a large combine.

This was also the time when I made my last serious attempt at poetry with a long philosophical poem in blank verse. There were occasional flashes of insight in it; for instance, after writing of man's insignificance when the whole earth on which he lives is no more than a speck of dust in the cosmos, I went on to refute this view by bringing in the conception of infinity, which dissolves differences of magnitude, being infinitely greater than the greatest as well as the least:

> Man is not small compared with the vast skies
> When, in the Infinite, is neither great nor small.

However it was not good poetry — fortunately not, because it would have been regrettable that one who was later to write from even theoretical understanding should have confused matters by first publishing his own unguided meanderings.

It was in 1932 that we set up house in Gdynia. I ought to have been ideally happy. I was ecstatically in love with my wife, and I had regular work again. The duties were light — only about half a day — and the salary adequate; in any case I supplemented it with lessons at a commercial school and a few private lessons. We had the sea in front and beautiful wooded hills behind. And yet I was restless and dissatisfied. The thought of life lengthening out into an endless drab vista of work and salary pressed down on me like claustrophobia. My father wrote advising me to get back to school in England, because every year I spent abroad was a year wasted from the point of view of increments on the Burnham scale and eventual pension; but that seemed an even more dismal prospect. I could not settle down; I wanted to go off on holidays alone; I laboured constantly at the writing of worthless novels and short stories. I felt inwardly bankrupt. I began to incline towards Communism, not for any intrinsic merit I found in it, but simply as a challenge to the sham world around me, not even investigating to see whether it also was not a sham. Christ said that he who seeks will find;

perhaps for one who does not even know that there is anything to seek, refusal to be satisfied with a meaningless life may be the equivalent of search.

A cultural Anglo-Polish Society was formed at Gdynia, which held weekly meetings and entertained tourists passing through the town and ships' officers calling there. I wrote and produced humorous one-act plays for it and in their success enjoyed a tawdry imitation of the literary fame I craved. For a while I acted as honorary secretary to the society and then it was decided that the amount of work had increased enough to justify a professional secretary. Four young men straight from Oxford held the post in succession while we were there, each staying about a year. The first of them was Martin Lings, who became a personal friend of ours. He was a slightly built man of medium height, with a Vandyke beard and a manner of grave courtesy behind which lay considerable firmness of character. After about a year he left to take up a post as English lecturer at the University of Kaunas in Lithuania.

7

The Quest Begins

IT WAS IN 1936, my thirtieth year, that the change of course set in. It was high time, because the ship of my life, drifting uncharted, had got into the shallows and almost run aground.

In February Catherine was born, our first child. In the summer Martin Lings came to stay with us on his way back from Lithuania, where he had just given up his job. He made the impression on me of having grown argumentative. He tried to prove the Renaissance had been a calamity, which, of course, led to a historical discussion. Then he told me his outlook on history and civilization, and indeed, on life itself, had been totally changed by reading the works of a writer who had complete knowledge. I objected that in modern times knowledge is far too extensive for one man to possess it all, and he explained that he did not mean detailed factual knowledge but integral or essential knowledge. I did not understand what he meant by that and he was unable to explain. Looking back now, it seems extraordinary that he should not have been able to tell us the

30   *My Life and Quest*

simple essence of what a spiritual outlook implies: the Oneness of Being and the possibility of Self-realization. Instead he asked me to read the books for myself. This I was not prepared to do. I was writing a novel and had no time at present, I told him. He left two books with me, asking me to read them when I found time, and I half promised to do so.

It was October before I got round to reading the books Martin had left for me. The one I took up first was a book of essays by Ouspensky. I still retained a critical mind and was by no means prepared to accept whatever ivory tower was offered as a refuge from a meaningless life. Some of the things he said interested me, but I made a list of dubious statements, contradictions and unjustified assumptions and sent it to Martin, saying that it was not even accurate or consistent, let alone complete knowledge. He wrote back with some humility, accepting my criticisms, admitting that he might have been wrong about Ouspensky, but asserting that it was the other writer whom he meant when he spoke about writing from knowledge.

The other was one of the early books of Rene Guenon, I think *Introduction generale a l'etude des doctrines Hindoues*. There was no question of criticism this time. From the very first page I drank it in like some one so parched with thirst that he absorbs moisture through the very pores of his skin. When I came to the sentence 'Being is One' I felt physically, in my heart, not as a brain-thought, "This is true. I have always known it was true but didn't know that I knew." That moment, a moment I still clearly envisage, sitting alone in the room, in an armchair in my flat in Gdynia, was the beginning of the quest which I was never again to relinquish, from which I was never to turn aside. For Guenon left no doubt that it was a quest. If it had been mere theory it would have not interested me, but the implication was kept well

Arthur Osborne 31

to the fore—Being is One; therefore you yourself cannot be other than the One Being, because there is no other; therefore to realize your true self is to realize the Supreme Identity with Absolute, Universal, Eternal Being: and this can be done.

So life had a meaning after all! It was not a mere inane trickle of events. My restlessness and discontent fell away. My ambition to become a writer evaporated. The goal and purpose of life was clear. Nevertheless a wave of caution rose up; I said to myself: "Are you prepared to undertake this? Remember that you are not psychic and do not have visions and ecstasy, and it means giving up pleasures that you know to be real for pleasures that may be real." And immediately the answer arose in my mind: "It is not a question of pleasure but truth; I have to follow it because it is true; truth is its own compulsion and I have no option."

Before carrying the story further I should say something about Guenon and his influence. In the second quarter of this century he wrote a series of books and numerous articles expounding the inner unanimity of the religions (or 'traditions', as he preferred to call them), the meaning of symbolism, the possibilities of initiatic training, and the true hierarchical basis of society or civilization. His teaching can be summarized as follows:

Being is One, and therefore by realizing your true Self you realize your identity with Divine, Universal Being. This is the essential teaching of all religions, although it may be proclaimed openly, as in the Eastern religions, or veiled and confined to esoteric societies, as in the Western. Therefore all religions are unanimous in their essence, although divergent and even incompatible in their more external applications, that is in doctrine, theology, ritual, and the social organization and code of conduct they sponsor. Every religion, so long as its full spiritual integrity remains, has initiatic organizations in which the aspirant can obtain guidance on the path towards ultimate Realization of the Supreme Identity. These organizations, in order to be valid, must descend in an unbroken chain from the origin, each guru (since the word 'guru' has been accepted into the English language as signifying 'spiritual guide', I use it for the sake of convenience in this book, whether it applies to a Hindu guide or any other) being appointed by his predecessor. What the aspirant has to do is to find a guru, no matter in what religion, who has both vertical and horizontal authenticity, that is to say, who is a realized man and also the validly appointed successor to a chain of gurus, and seek initiation and guidance from him. However, having chosen any religion, he must follow it scrupulously in its outer organization of life and worship, its ritual and observances and moral code, as well as its more essential teaching, since each religion is an organic whole.

This for the individual, but for the organization of mankind in society he taught no less emphatically that normally and traditionally a spiritual purpose underlies, and a spiritual authority controls, the whole of civilization. Any civilization which breaks away from its spiritual roots and bases itself on rationalist and materialist values is a monstrosity and cannot have stability or endure for long. Therefore our modern civilization, far from being the highest achievement of mankind, is an aberration foredoomed to destruction by its very nature, while our modern sciences consist of such knowledge as traditional civilizations would not have thought worthwhile accumulating, since they have no spiritual basis and do not further the spiritual development of those who acquire them.

All this he expounds with brilliant lucidity, vast erudition, and unshakable conviction that he was right and scathing contempt for all who disagreed.

Arthur Osborne 33

He usually was right but not always. For instance, he asserted that no Hindu believes in reincarnation, which he declared to be a travesty of Hinduism invented by modern Western misinterpreters. Even more serious — he dismissed Buddhism as a spurious religion. Bearing in mind his axiom that there is no neutrality in religion, that everything is initiatic or counter-initiatic or in plainer language, of divine or satanic origin, this implies the assumption that the whole of Buddhism, with all its saints and poets, its Arhats and Bodhisattvas is based on error and evil. He admitted, indeed, that such Buddhist currents as had passed through China had been purified and spiritualized by the Chinese influence, but this involved the assumption that the Chinese sages had chosen a satanic vehicle into which to pour their influence!

Before the end of his life he did indeed retract this error, though without admitting that he had previously made it and even then insofar as concerned Mahayana, which he declared, in defiance of history, to be the original Buddhism.

Strangely enough, even errors of this magnitude did little to impair the value of his work. So vast was its sweep, such an affirmation of truth pervaded it, that errors seemed swallowed up in the sea of truth. Not that any of us would have admitted at that time that there were errors. Even though there were, they were due to his faulty application of the principles he proclaimed, whereas the merit of his work was that he did proclaim true principles on which to base the conduct of life, the understanding of its meaning and the judgement of a civilization, instead of personal ideas and prejudices.

His influence was less widespread than his clear insight, lucid exposition and vast erudition would have justified. Perhaps this was due to his extreme militancy and refusal to compromise. For instance, an orientalist who felt vaguely the sublimity of the ancient texts he was handling, without however grasping their meaning and implications with the clarity which Guenon demanded (and there have been many such) would not be disposed to learn from one who dismissed his whole science as 'learned ignorance'. Similarly, a psychologist who was prepared to admit spiritual springs to men's actions could obviously not express agreement with a writer who denounced modern psychology *in toto* as of 'counter-initiatic', by which he meant 'satanic', origin. Even social, political and economic reformers would find little common ground with one who denounced not merely this or that aspect of modernism but modern civilization as a whole, root and branch.

However, what his influence lost in scope it gained in profundity, for those who did accept his teaching did so whole-heartedly, many of them indeed, changing not merely their outlook but their whole attitude to life. And in the course of time some of them also began to write and to exert an influence in less tangible ways, thus carrying forward the influence that Guenon had originated.

For myself, I was predisposed to accept his teaching as regarded civilization no less than the meaning and the purpose of life for the individual, since, as I have already said, I had intuitively revolted against the mechanism, materialism and vulgarity of our age and had never really reconciled myself to it. Now at last I had the doctrinal justification of what I had long felt intuitively.

How far did the impact of Guenon immediately change me, and how far did it merely set in motion a lengthy process of change? The theory of conversion changing a man's nature in a twinkling, as held in some Protestant sects, is too facile. Deep-rooted tendencies and predispositions are not so easily eradicated.

Arthur Osborne 35

Only in the rarest cases, when a man is already concentrated and already, without knowing it, ripe for self-surrender, will a single mental conviction, a single vision, or even a single flash of realization (as in the case of the Maharshi) suffice to effect an immediate and permanent change. Normally the most it can do is to turn his mind in a new direction and convince him of the necessity of working to achieve the permanent change.

As for myself, it is necessary to differentiate between what were weaknesses of character and what were mere symptoms of frustration. The latter disappeared naturally with the eradication of their cause, the former had to be fought; and it was a long and arduous fight. And when I say that I never relinquished the quest or turned aside from it, that only means that I never doubted and never ceased to aim at the one goal; it does not mean that no harmful thoughts or wrong actions due to weakness of character ever intervened to create unnecessary difficulties on the path. They did only too often.

To be more specific: the desire to be a famous writer, the horror of routine professional existence, the inclination to Communism and the longing to go off alone faded out naturally, not being qualities of character but merely symptoms of revolt against the meaningless life which I had hitherto faced. On the other hand, I was a very conceited young man and the quality of conceit, instead of being eradicated, was simply transplanted from my own supposed abilities to the truth of which I was now aware while others were not. Indeed, a certain arrogance which, in Guenon, might be the impersonal arrogance of truth towards error, was apt to infect even disciples who were less inclined that way by nature than I was. Like so many new converts, I was agog with enthusiasm to convert others. Basically this was a warm-hearted eagerness to share with them the new wealth I had discovered, but it was tainted also with conceit, with the desire to prevail in argument and prove myself right. It would not be true to say that I proselytised indiscriminately — for instance, I did not try to do so with my colleagues or students at the college where I taught; but whenever I met any one who seemed able to understand I would try in some way or other to draw him into an argument, quite confident of my superior artillery and skill in using it once the argument started.

I also sent Guenon books to the few friends who I thought would understand. I sent *The Symbolism of the Cross* to Morgan. A few months later, when we were in England and I called on him, he simply said that he thought it able but not quite sound. I sent one (I forget which) to Rosamond and she wrote back that it was a nice book. Furious at such faint praise, I wrote her a scathing reply, but it was really I who was at fault. I ought to have sent her a careful and detailed explanation of what it all meant and then followed this up with one of the more elementary books. Perhaps I had the same inability at this time as Martin to give a simple explanation. Truth is simple, only men's minds are complicated and seek complexity.

It was through Martin that my wife and I were drawn to Guenon and thereby indirectly to Bhagavan. Perhaps one cannot know what people will understand or, even if they show initial understanding, pursue the path to a good end. If a man's life really rests on a spiritual basis, some air of serenity and power will radiate from him and draw those who are interested to seek guidance even without argument; that is to say, if it is his nature and destiny to influence people in this particular way, by drawing outsiders into the circle. A Master may feel who are his people and draw them to himself, but even that is no guarantee that they will overcome evil: Judas was among the close followers of

Arthur Osborne 37

Christ and Devadatta among those of Buddha. And Mohammad was told: "You cannot save whom you will but whom God wills." It has nothing to do with intellectual ability as commonly understood. A great scientist can fail to understand spiritual science, denying it altogether or having merely the exoteric faith of the simple churchgoer, or getting caught up in some freak occultism; a philosopher can be receptive to the Perennial Philosophy, reading spiritual texts without grasping their implication; a psychologist can remain ignorant of what underlies the mind. On the other hand, a spiritual master need not be an intellectual. Ramakrishna had the mind rather of a peasant than a philosopher. And Ignatius Loyola was temperamentally so averse to study that it required an immense effort for him to take his degree, and he was middle-aged before he did so.

It is also not a question of any special faculty comparable, for instance, to that for art or music. It is not a question of being psychic. There is nothing spiritual in psychic powers or in most that are called occultism and spiritualism, while, on the other hand, people who are not psychic can understand and take the quest. Psychic ability may be a help at certain stages of some types of path, but it is more likely to be a danger, since it can open the mind to various allurements which have to be left behind, like the sirens whom Oddyseus heard but against whom he made his crew plug their ears. If the pleasure of the physical world is seductive and hard to renounce, those of the subtle world are certainly no less so. Christ said that if a man attains to the kingdom of heaven all else shall be given him in addition; but that is after attaining. If he seeks all else beforehand, he is not likely to attain. It is safer to have one's ears plugged.

It might be said that what is required is willingness to open one's heart to the truth, in fact to surrender oneself, to give up one's ego, to conceive of the possibility of its non-existence. That is why the *Quran* speaks of unbelievers rather as perverse than ignorant, saying of them that even if an angel came down from heaven to explain to them, they would not listen.

From this it might be supposed that those who do understand and take the quest should be people of uncommon goodness, strikingly free from egoism. Some are, no doubt, and it is they who are on a good way, because, whatever the religion and whatever the path followed, it is a path towards liquidation of the ego, the individual 'I'-consciousness with all its fears and cravings, its grudges and pettiness, and therefore the goal obviously cannot be attained while building up or even retaining the ego. However, it is by no means always so. In fact, many who take the path, many members of spiritual groups, will be found to be more egoistic than those one would be likely to meet in some group of people united for worldly or social ends — more jealous, more ungoverned, quicker to take offence, less generous, less inclined to give in. This is likely to come as a shock and disillusionment to one joining such a group.

One explanation that is given is that spiritual training (as is claimed also for certain types of psychiatric treatment) squeezes out the lower tendencies in a man, of which he himself was perhaps unaware, bringing them to the surface and thereby making them temporarily more obtrusive, so that an aggravation is a stage in the cure. When a devotee complained to the Maharshi that other thoughts arose more forcibly when he tried to meditate, he replied: "Yes, all kinds of thoughts arise in meditation. That is only right, for what is hidden in you is brought out. Unless it rises up how can it be destroyed? Thoughts rise up spontaneously, but only to be extinguished in due course, thus strengthening the mind." (*The*

Arthur Osborne 39

Teachings of Ramana Maharshi in His Own Words, Ch. 5). Once when people complained to him of the arrogant behaviour of an old devotee he replied: "That is his *vasanas* (inherent tendencies) coming out." When a person first understands and sets forth on the spiritual quest one may see a new radiance overspread him, a sort of foreshadowing of his perfected state, making him altogether delightful. However, this will not last. It will be followed by a stage when all his lowest possibilities come to the surface and he seems to be worse than before. At this time patience is needed. However, this stage is also temporary, and therefore this cannot be the full explanation of the egoistic types that are often found in a spiritual circle, at any rate such of them as were arch-egoists before taking the path and remain so afterwards.

When Christ was accused of associating with riff-raff his reply was that it is those who are sick that need a doctor, not those who are well. There was probably a good deal of sarcasm in this reply (for Christ also was an extremely militant teacher and verbally he hit back hard when attacked); it can hardly be taken at its face value, because only those who have attained the goal are really well, certainly not the smugly self-satisfied who could ask such a question. However, it does indicate that it is often the misfits, those who have failed to adapt themselves to life, who recognize that they are sick and seek treatment. When the Maharshi was asked why we should seek Self-realization he would sometimes answer: "Who asks you if you are satisfied with life as it is?" When asked what use it is, he replied: "Why do you seek Self-realization? Why don't you rest content with your present state? It is evident that you are discontented and your discontent will come to an end if you realize your Self." (*ibid,* Ch.7). This explains why it is the discontented who seek, but not why so many of them are unpleasant persons.

It may be because the quest offers much for the ego to grasp at. This may seem a surprising statement when its whole purpose is the liquidation of the ego, and yet it is true. Man in his present state possesses only a small part of his potential powers and perceptions. The process which goes on, often unconsciously, during the quest is a twofold process of expansion and contraction, symbolized by Jupiter and Saturn, expanding a man's faculties while at the same time crushing him to the point of 'self-naughting', as the mediaeval Christian mystics put it. Christ said that a man must lose his life in order to gain it and that when a man attains the kingdom of heaven all else shall be added to him. This represents two successive stages: first contraction of the ego to nothingness and then infinite expansion. But in actual practise the two processes are seldom so clearly divided. The adding and subtraction or expansion and squeezing go on side-by-side; and that is the trouble. An aspirant may go through alternate phases of expansion, when grace floods his heart and the quest is a lilt of beauty, and contraction when he seems to have lost everything and be squeezed to the bones, when all is dryness and he is tempted to despond and can do nothing but grit his teeth and hold on with grim perseverance. But there is also the danger that the process of expansion may take the form of new powers and perceptions on the subtle plane which is likely to seduce him from his path, as Circe or the lotus-eaters did the comrades of Odysseus. Like Circe, they may also turn their victims into swine. A true guru will encourage no such things. Let them come after the kingdom of heaven has been attained, as Christ said. The Maharshi cautioned that even when powers come unsought they should not be accepted. They are like a rope to tether a horse. Indeed, reference to them as a goal or reward of the quest is always a suspicious sign in a guru. Even

Arthur Osborne 41

without full knowledge, the ego has a premonition of the delicious fruits dangling on the trees ahead.

It is also a premonition of its own impending sacrifice. The premonition of expansion explains the many who are called and the queer company they are; the need for contraction explains the few that are chosen. The combination of the two processes explains the nervous tension that is often set up when, instead of complementary, they become opposing forces. It is no play-acting and no easy task. There will be no success until the ego is prepared to surrender and go to its own sacrifice, but on the way it may pass the trees I referred to, dangling with tempting but unearned fruits. The conflict between the two tendencies may be enough to overbalance the mind. I have seen such cases and at the least this kind of madness is always egoism pushed beyond the limits.

The question who can understand the supreme Goal and dedicate his life to its quest is, of course, not the same as the question who can read Guenon. At first I thought it was. In fact, I divided mankind quite simply into those who had read and understood Guenon and those who had not. Actually, of course, there are people who can approach the Truth but not through that gateway. I was driven to recognize this because my wife was one such. I never for a moment doubted her ability to understand, and I was therefore dismayed when she would not read Guenon. She simply said that she could not read a whole chapter about what could be said in a few sentences. Although I did not appreciate it, she was of a more intuitive type, more the artist and less the scholar. Perhaps women in general tend to be; but one cannot generalize too far in this matter; I have known women who come to the path through Guenon and men who have needed a more direct or intuitive

42 *My Life and Quest*

approach. In any case, my wife followed mainly through my explanations but without full conviction or wholehearted dedication. Only later, when she came to the Maharshi, the sheer power of his presence, the grace and beauty that shone in him, a single prolonged gaze from his resplendent eyes, was enough to remove all doubt, with no word spoken. Thenceforth she was as devoted as any. There also she found books which really did say things in a sentence, books such as the *Avadhuta Gita* and the poems of Thayumanavar, and became proficient in theory also until she could distinguish true teaching from false as clearly as any follower of Guenon.

As for me, I flung myself ravenously on Guenon's books, I subscribed to the French monthly in which he wrote and also obtained all the back numbers that were available. I devoured whatever books I could lay hands on, either in English or French, dealing with mysticism, esoterism, symbolism, no matter of what religion. Not only did I read but study. I kept an alphabetical card index on my writing desk, as my tutors had done at Oxford, with a card for each name, theme or subject, noting down allusions, references and information as I read.

According to strict Guenon theory, I am not right in saying that the quest began for me at this time, because he taught that it begins with initiation; and he himself was not a guru and did not give initiation. Nevertheless, I am convinced that some spiritual influence flowed from him to those who read his books and re-directed their lives accordingly. In any case the mere fact of changing from an aimless, dissatisfied life to one directed consciously towards the supreme goal was bound to make an enormous difference.

Egoistical thoughts and actions might continue, but they were disapproved of; there was a constant struggle against them.

Arthur Osborne 43

A series of symbolical dreams bore witness to the inner change that was taking place. First there was a rectification of what the psychologists call the 'flight from fear', although I had not yet heard of it. The recollection came to me that in boyhood I had sometimes had dreams (not the same recurrent dream), which had threatened to turn into nightmare, but had avoided the frightening part by waking up. I felt that this had been the beginning of my loss of integrity and that I must go back into them and see them through to the end. When I determined to do so I found, to my surprise, that there was in fact nothing very terrible. It was only the determination that was needed. After that there were other symbolical dreams, such as a person gets at an important turning point in his life. Some of them brought before me the realization that the first stage of my route was a return to the comparative integrity of Oxford.

A person's whole life is a path he treads, leading to the ordained end. If at some point it becomes consciously so, that is the great blessing which makes achievement at least an envisaged goal. In my case, before that could happen, I had to come down to the nadir, to an inner destitution where all hope seemed to have failed and all values become hollow; not a state of spiritual poverty, because there was no humility in it, nor of financial poverty, but of what might be called enforced poverty of life. The moment I reached the nadir Grace was manifested in a form making re-ascent possible, but this happened in two stages. To·prevent my rushing onward to disintegration came my marriage, a foreshadowing of Divine Grace, with its recall to happiness, integrity and aspiration and a return to professional work. However, even such an influence was too weak to arrest the trend, with the result that the current was flowing both ways, re-ascent and continued descent, a new purpose in life and an inner bankruptcy and lack of purpose, until Grace was manifested anew with my discovery of Guenon. If that was the first act in the drama of the quest, my marriage was the prologue to it.

8

Adventures on the Path

A SMALL GROUP of us came to Guenon at the same time; I think the others were all younger than myself and all unmarried. I was to meet one and another of them under various circumstances on the path, but at the time I knew only Martin, or had just met two others as visitors to him. He, I think, knew them all. I do not mean a group in any organic sense, for that we never were — the only grouping Guenon would have approved of was that of guru and disciples. Just a number of people who were drawn from the circumference towards the centre at the same time and in the same way.

Read with understanding, Malory's 'Morte d'Arthur' is a very sad story. The whole noble company of knights were gathered together at Arthur's court for the feast of Pentecost, and while they were seated at the Round Table the Sangraal passed through the hall on a beam of light, but veiled so that none actually saw it. They were asked who would undertake its quest and all alike pledged themselves and rode forth with

46   *My Life and Quest*

courage and high hope. Some, however, soon turned back, finding the tug of the world too strong; some perished by the way; some were daunted or overthrown by the dragons of the ego; some bewitched or cast into dungeons by enchanters, the false guides who beset the path; some turned aside to lesser adventures or settled down in castles along the way; some attained a single vision of the Sangraal and recognized that, for them, that was sufficient achievement for this lifetime; and out of all that noble company only three pursued the quest to the end.

Guenon had said that the only thing to be done was to find a guru, in any religion, who had both horizontal and vertical authenticity, that is to say who was both the validly appointed successor to an initiatic chain and a realized man, and to seek initiation and guidance from him. Therefore it was a matter of mere expedience to us what religion we joined. It simply depended where we could find a guru — an easy matter, we thought then, in our simplicity. However, he had also said he had failed to find any Christian organization which still combined full theoretical understanding with spiritual potency; and therefore we decided that it would be necessary to look farther afield. Technically he may have been right, and certainly my earlier failure to find an opening in Christianity inclined me to accept his verdict; however it may be possible to attach too much importance to technical considerations in spiritual life and not enough to the Grace that bloweth where it listeth. Later I was to come upon evidence of spiritual currents in the Christian West, some of whose representatives seemed by no means inferior in power and understanding to Westerners who had transplanted themselves to Eastern religions. Nor were such signs of life confined to the Catholic Church, to which alone Guenon would allow some technical legitimacy. In view of this it does not seem absolutely necessary for Western aspirants in general to seek a path outside their ancestral religion and even less so to take on themselves the burden of a foreign orthodoxy. It is, moreover, to be remembered that the spiritual power of any religion or church is not a fixed quantum but a living, vibrating force, continually radiating with greater or less intensity, attaining an incandescent heat or cooling down and growing inert, according to the fervour and sincerity and understanding of those within its orbit. And since every thought, every action, every aspiration has its repercussions, those who draw sustenance from a spiritual body thereby also increase its potency, while the reverse is also true, but those who devote their lives to its services, asking no reward, thereby draw sustenance.

Some undoubtedly will be drawn to an eastern religion or to the formless path of Self-enquiry which will be described later in this book, and this cannot be considered regrettable. The characteristic of our age being the mutual acquaintance of doctrines and paths which had previously remained isolated, it is a good thing that those of the East should have representatives in the West to temper the obtuseness and smug superiority to which the Western intellect is so prone. On a more profound level also, the existence of various spiritual currents side by side cannot but increase the present fermentation and renewal of spiritual life. For this is a time of renewal: even more, it is a time of division between those who have completely rejected the mild religious restraints of their ancestors and those who seek something more vital with fuller understanding and stronger purpose.

And about myself? If I had learnt of the life and testimony of the Christian mystics and came upon their modern followers when I was searching so vainly at Oxford, should I have found a home there and avoided the ten barren, wasteful years that were to follow before I discovered Guenon? Such a hypothetical question is always unreal, since things could not really have happened otherwise than they did. Certain it is that it was only Guenon's mode of expression which could fully satisfy my intellect, and, much as I revere the beauty and profundity of the various paths, Christian, Islamic and others, only the quintessential doctrine of Non-duality and the Maharshi's path of Self-enquiry based upon it corresponded with my needs and temperament and offered me perfect fulfilment.

Moreover, people's destinies are so interwoven as to make any might-have-been illusory. If I had found an opening in England I should not have drifted to Poland and therefore not to have met my wife and snatched her, from the chaos that Europe was to become, to Arunachala, at the feet of the Maharshi, where she also was to find the only fulfilment this life could offer.

At that time, however, I, like the others of our group, took Guenon's verdict unquestioning and simply presumed that it was necessary to abandon Christianity and seek farther afield. I could not avoid a feeling of regret that, whereas the others were all free to go to the East in search of a guru, being unmarried and for the most part, sufficiently well-to-do, I had no prospect of leaving Europe. However, as it turned out, within a year I was in the East while many or most of them were still in the West.

A person's destiny is not an accident. It is not something extraneous to him. From one point of view it is the outcome of his thoughts and actions, an inevitable, automatic system of repercussions which can be called reward and retribution, and from another point of view the milieu necessary for his development. What obscures this from sight is the wrong habit

Arthur Osborne 49

of considering worldly happiness or prosperity the purpose of
life, whereas it may often happen that the reverse is what a man's
development needs. It is understandable, therefore, that once a
man has recognized Self-realization as his conscious goal and
turned in that direction, his destiny should become more
recognizably beneficent and meaningful, even though it may
involve hardship.

After four years at the Maritime College I left Poland for
Bangkok where I took up the post of lecturer in English at the
Chulalongkorn University. Having taken a degree in one subject
and drifted into teaching of another created difficulties in my
academic career. This proved a blessing in disguise in our case as
it prevented us from being caught up by the Nazis in Poland a
few years later or by the Communists in Lithuania. In one way
or another all the members of our little group were brought
safely through the war. The lower reality of events does not
condition but subserves the higher reality of the quest. That
does not mean that no one who has dedicated himself to the
quest can die before its conclusion but that his worldly success
or failure, prosperity or privation, even life or death, will be
such as his progress on the quest demands.

I liked Siam, as I had liked Oxford. I liked the Siamese — a
cheerful, easy-going, friendly people; and yet Siam was the
second great wave of disappointment to me, as Oxford had
been the first. I had built up a dream-picture of Oxford which
the reality could not substantiate; I had come to Siam imbued
with Guenon's descriptions of the traditional East, where
political and social conditions subserve the spiritual discipline,
where authority rests, openly or secretly, with the guardians of
tradition, where the quest of Realization is recognized as the
goal and the purpose of life; and instead I found a nation

tumbling over itself to acquire the materialist civilization which I was trying to discard, and flinging away with both hands that to which I had dedicated my life, turning their back on it, trying to forget that it had ever existed. I had already known one Siamese, Seni Pramoj, a great-nephew of King Chulalongkorn, after whom the university was called, who was Siamese Minister in Washington during the Second World War and Prime Minister after the war; he had been Denzil Batchelor's room-mate at Oxford. He was a dapper, practical little man whose great interest in life was tennis and he thought Denzil and I mad for our preoccupation with poetry and ideas. He was typical of his people.

Even before the quest started I had found kindred souls in England opposed to modern civilization with its materialist values, its divorce from nature, its rush and noise and superficiality. But when I got to Poland I found the viewpoint of Eastern Europe was quite different. There modernism and industrialization still had a glamour. The term of contempt for a slum, for anything dirty or old-fashioned, was 'Asia', while the national pride was a coalmine or a steel foundry. If I even mentioned my viewpoint I encountered the suspicion that I was the cunning Englishman who, having industrialization in his own country, was trying to beguile East Europeans into putting up with backwardness in theirs. I was to find the same spirit in the East. In fact, I was to find that it was in the West, among those surfeited with materialism, that the renewed search for spiritual meaning was arising, while the East was rushing headlong into modernism.

I found that even the traditional arts and sciences, about which Guenon wrote so much, were disappearing. The last generation of Siamese architects had refused to initiate apprentices, saying that the age of tradition was ended. As a result, modern buildings in the Siamese style, such as the university in which I taught, were mere imitations planned by Italian architects.

True, there were the Buddhist monasteries in Siam, and I might have made a more careful investigation of them, but so far as I could gather from talks with my students and colleagues there was no very potent spiritual current there. Yes, there had been a Buddhist monk in the north who was said to be very holy and many people had visited him, but he was dead now. No, there was no one else. Incidentally, I recently saw, as a sort of confirmation, on reading *The Wheel of Life*, the autobiography of my postwar successor at the university, John Blofeld, who is a Buddhist, that he found no living current in Siamese Buddhism but had had to go to Sikkim to seek a guru.

Guenon's description of the East, I found, would have been idealized and doctrinaire even in an earlier age; today it simply would not apply.

We soon heard from Martin that he had taken up a post as English lecturer at Cairo University. Guenon also was living at Cairo and Martin got to know him and gradually became a sort of unofficial secretary to him.

Before long Martin wrote to us that he had found a Muslim guru, approved of by Guenon, became a Muslim, and had been initiated by him. He also expressed the opinion that we should probably eventually be driven to join the same religion and even to follow the same guru.

With Guenon's approval, our group had undertaken the translation of his books, each selecting one. Martin was translating *Orient et Occident* and I its sequel, *La Crise du Monde Modern* which appealed to me as a beautiful, condensed and fundamental work. I finished the translation just before the war spread to the East, and I am told that Luzac published it under the title *The Modern Crisis*. I never saw a copy; I was cut off by the war at the time, and later I never troubled to get one.

One of the benefits of this work was that it enabled us to correspond with Guenon, who was very punctilious about the details of translation and about preserving his long sentences and careful system of punctuation. In the periodical for which he wrote he had inserted an announcement that he could not answer personal letters or give advice or guidance. Perhaps this was necessary to avert a flood of correspondence in answering questions and explaining points of difficulty.

I took advantage of this correspondence to tell him of the disappointment I had experienced from the contrast of the present reality of Siam with his idealized picture of the East, and it was partly as a result of my representation that he, or Martin Lings for him, explained in the English translation of *Orient et Occident* that eastern countries of today do not correspond with his description of the traditional East. Such an explanation was, however, inadequate; the books should have been revised throughout to make it clear that it was not the East as it is that was being described but an ideal.

Driven by impatience, I followed Martin's example in becoming a Muslim. In my case, however, this ran rather counter to Guenon's injunction that one should first find a valid guru before making a change of religion. It might be said that I had indirectly found the one followed by Martin of whom I was told that Guenon approved; however, especially in view of the war, there was no knowing how long it would be before I was able to approach him directly; and if I had meanwhile discovered

Arthur Osborne 53

a Buddhist or Hindu or Taoist guru it might have put me in an awkward position of having to change my religion a second time. Theoretically, if I required any emotional support before finding a valid guru, I should have sought it in the religion in which I had been brought up. In actual fact, however, it would have been hard to revive a jaded piety, whereas I did find immense support in Islam.

In Bangkok, I appreciated the occasional evenings of Arabic song and incantation that my South Indian Muslim friends held in a large hall above a cloth merchant's offices. There is one of these that still rings in my head at times. In translation it would be: "I ask pardon of God for what (in me) is not God; and all things say 'God'!" The first phrase is an enunciation of pure non-duality, of the Supreme Identity, regarding all 'otherness', all separate individuality (or illusion of it) in oneself as a sin for which to ask forgiveness. This is, in its deepest sense, the sin of *shirk*, of associating any 'other' with God, which is described in Islam as the one unforgivable sin— naturally, because when this is finally overcome there remains no other-than-God and therefore no sin or sinner to forgive. The second phrase describes the entire utterance of the name of God. And the men who spent their evenings in this manner were neither scholars nor men dedicated to the spiritual quest but simple merchants. It was amazing and very refreshing to feel the warmth and depth of their faith and to see the naturalness with which they regarded their religion as an absorbing reality and a constant topic of conversation, so unlike either the normal Western indifference or the truculent assertiveness often found in those who are religious. Here at last I was coming in contact with the traditional East, even though their standards may have fallen far short of what tradition demanded. Theoretically at least they recognized

54 *My Life and Quest*

the supreme goal, as the incantation translated above testifies. In practise they received initiation and followed a discipline though without full understanding or complete dedication. Even among them some of the younger generation were becoming lax both in life and worship.

I began harmonising my breathing with my pulse beat. With a little practise it is easy to feel one's pulse internally without putting one's finger on any spot; and harmonising it with the breathing helps to rhythmetise one. When walking I kept my footsteps also to the same rhythm. To enhance the vibration it is very helpful to repeat silently a mantra, a ceaseless inner prayer attuned to the breathing and heartbeat like 'Arunachala Siva' or simply 'Om'. In Islam one would repeat the *shahada*, the Islamic confession of faith, silently — 'there is no god' while breathing out and 'except God' while breathing in — so that every exhalation becomes a denial of the ego and every inhalation an assertion of the One Self.

Years later I discovered from reading that this was a form of the ceaseless inner prayer, which in one form or another, is practised in all religions. Perhaps the best-known illustration of it is the constant prayer 'Lord Jesus Christ, have mercy on me', also attuned to the breathing and heartbeat, used by an anonymous Russian pilgrim, as described in *The Way of the Pilgrim* (English translation by R.M. French, SPCK). It may not suit all wayfarers or every path. At that stage of the path it was most useful to me. It maintained a living spiritual rhythm and also helped to guard against sins of forgetfulness.

There is no rigid barrier between the physical and spiritual. The spiritual current can be kept up during our daily activities as a sort of substratum and then the work performed will not only not suffer but will go on more effectively because it will be

Arthur Osborne 55

more spontaneous. Rhythmic movements during prayers, prostrations and rituals emphasize this and one may feel intuitively the need to extend the rhythmetisation to the body also. Indeed, mental, moral and physical harmonisation is the threefold basis of spiritual development. It is true that physical harmonisation alone does not lead to spiritual growth, but neither does mental understanding alone nor moral rectitude alone; it is the combination of the three that is needed. On the direct path, total harmonisation is produced spontaneously and such disciplines leading to it can be ignored; but that was a path to which I had not yet been led.

Early in 1939 news came that two of our group, who had been travelling about in India for some time, had at last found a guru. It is easy to remember the date, because it was less than a fortnight after the birth of our son that my summer vacation started, and my wife, knowing how much it meant to me, raised no objection to my going.

As soon as I reached India I had the peculiar feeling of being at home for the first time in my life. I had never felt really at home in England but had always intended to make my living abroad. Neither had I felt at home in Poland or Siam. It was not that I preferred the Indians — indeed, the gay cheerfulness of the Chinese shopkeepers in Bangkok was something I missed in the Indian shops. Nor were the parts of India I then visited particularly beautiful — dusty, sun-bleached plains, dilapidated villages, bleak, white-washed houses. There was simply the indefinable feeling that I belonged here, that this was home.

I stayed in a middle-class hotel in a hot, white-walled, dusty town through the worst of the summer heat. A single-storey hotel, no fans, very cheap by European standards. I shared a room with my two friends — I had not met them before but

56   *My Life and Quest*

they immediately became friends, companions on the quest. There is a *hadith*, a saying of the Prophet: "There is no friendship but only companionship-in-Islam." At night we and our neighbours in the hotel took our beds out into the courtyard to sleep — the Indian *charpoy*, a light wooden framework with cord criss-crossed between it and a mattress only about an inch thick thrown over.

I adapted myself easily, and here again I appreciated the atmosphere: mostly business and professional men — no women as far as I could see — many of the men devotional, most of them imbued with pride of Islam. They never doubted that it was the finest of all religions. Naïve? But does a Christian professor of comparative religion or a Buddhist abbot ever doubt that his is the finest religion? And is this not equally naïve? However, on the contingent level of dogma and social application the religions necessarily differ, like the sides of a mountain. Each represents a different viewpoint, and therefore each must seem best when seen *from its own viewpoint* and *from this viewpoint* every other must seem either wrong or at best inferior.

On the purely spiritual level all religions are unanimous. They cannot be otherwise, since Truth is One. It is like a mountain approached from different sides; the nature of the terrain differs on every side, and the paths run in different and even opposite directions, but the peak is one and they all converge on it. This is beginning to be widely appreciated nowadays and there have been a number of books either expounding it or illustrating it by means of comparative quotations culled from the mystics of the various religions.

What is needed is simply to attend to one's own religion or to see each from its own viewpoint. Throughout most of history the former has been the preferable attitude: so long as one sincerely followed one's own religion it was quite unnecessary

Arthur Osborne 57

to know about any other. The average Christian, for example, hardly knew that there was a religion called Buddhism, so why should he study it? Today however, with the expansion of a uniform modernism over all the religions and over the previously diverse civilizations which they sponsored, such an attitude is rarely possible for the intelligent and enquiring. Too much is known about the existence and surface disagreements of other religions. Therefore the second attitude becomes necessary for many people: to understand and explain each from its own viewpoint. Those who claim to be authorities on religion should facilitate this process, not obstruct it, as they so often do. Because if it is not done, the observer is faced with the dilemma that all the millions of followers of another religion affirm what his own denies and deny what it affirms. Simply to brush the problem aside by saying: "We are right and all the others are wrong" is too superficial an attitude to hold the intelligent student.

As an example of what I mean by viewpoint, there is an able and learned book by F.H.Hilliard called *The Buddha, the Prophet and the Christ* (Allen & Unwin) which examines the views of their followers on the divinity of these three founders of religions. It is more fair-minded and impartial than most such books; nevertheless it must inevitably suggest the superiority of that religion which is based on belief in the divinity of the Personal Saviour, that is to say Christianity. From the Islamic viewpoint the essential comparison would be between the *Quran*, the Gospels and the Pali Canon, and the scales would come down in favour of the only one of the three religions which is based on a divinely revealed scripture, that is Islam. From a Buddhist viewpoint it might be a comparison between the Noble Eightfold Path, Christ's injunctions to his followers and the Islamic *shariah*, and Buddhism would come first as the only one

58 *My Life and Quest*

of the three religions whose founder had himself laid down a clearly formulated path from suffering to Beatitude, from ignorance to Light, from *samsara* to Nirvana. Obviously, then, a really useful and instructive comparison would be one which showed the equivalence of personal saviour, revealed scripture and clearly demarcated path; and such a study would not need to grade the religions but to simply indicate the different modes of approach.

I was taken to see the guru (or *murshid*) in the cool cloister of an old stone house, looking out on a dusty courtyard. He kept me waiting a few minutes before entering: a short, broad man of about sixty, white-haired, bearded and bright eyed, with a brisk, alert manner and a look of keen intelligence. He was wearing a skullcap, gown and pyjama trousers, all of gleaming white cotton, freshly laundered and ironed. It was always so that I saw him. He asked general questions about my life, my work, my circumstances, touching on nothing spiritual. I felt a strong wave of disappointment. I had no impression of spirituality but put it down to my lack of psychic receptivity — the spiritual power must be there or my friends would not have recognized it. One of them, after two years ineffectual search, when he heard of this *murshid* had cancelled his ticket. The other had met Martin's guru but was more attracted to this one. Neither had any doubts.

It was some days before I received initiation. One day, during this interval, I was alone in the hotel when two of our neighbours came across to speak with me, professional men of about my age. After speaking about the pure doctrine of non-duality (which so many Indian Muslims, imbued with Sufi teachings, understand as clearly as Hindus) they suggested to me in a tactful way that I might not be very wise in my choice of

Arthur Osborne 59

a *murshid* and showed me a pamphlet in English by their own. I was not impressed by it and disliked his transliterating his name in such a way as to make it look English. Nor did I approve of their proselytising for a guru. I decided that rivalry was at the base of their warning and ignored it. In fact, I willed myself to believe in my *murshid* just as I had willed myself to be tragically in love at Oxford. Simplicity and sincerity are seldom natural qualities; they have to be acquired.

It was not into one Sufi order alone that I was initiated but into the group of great Indian Muslim orders, my *murshid* being entitled to represent them all. The spiritual exercises I was given are such as are only revealed on initiation; there was, however, one meditation among them which there is no harm and some interest in speaking about. There is a verse in the *Quran:* "He is now as He was"; and I was to meditate on the two in conjunction. If there was God alone and if He remains as He was, utterly unchanged, if the creation of the universe and all that it contains has not limited Him in any way, has not touched even the fringe of His Being, then all other-than-God is an appearance without intrinsic reality; He alone is the Real. Therefore whatever is the essence or reality of me cannot be other-than-God. I cannot say "I am God" but I can say "I am not other-than-God"; there is an enormous difference, for the former might deify the ego, the individual in me, while the latter denies its very existence; and when all the illusory other-than-God is denied, what remains? Only God, Who is now as He was.

This is a good example of how the Sufi saints read the highest meaning into the *Quran* and the sayings of the Prophet. There have been Western scholars who have questioned their right to do so, maintaining that no such meaning was intended. This is preposterous. What it comes to is the implication that

60   *My Life and Quest*

men whose whole lives are a quest for Truth, some of whom have attained the supreme super-rational Truth, have built their work on a foundation of error or falsification; also that the founder of one of the world's great religions had himself not seen beyond the exoteric wall to the deeper meaning of his message. It is ignorance criticising knowledge. People who do not understand the universal truth, even in theory, but look upon Sufism as a mere set of philosophical ideas may accept such a view, but not those who have understood that Truth is one and universal.

Why, then, is the truth of non-duality not explicitly taught in Islam, as it is in many Hindu and Buddhist texts? Why should it be necessary to seek it in hidden and symbolical sentences? A religion has to be adapted to an entire people, not only to a spiritual minority, and the type of adaptation required varies from the age and community. The various religious traditions teach that there is a process of diminishing spirituality in the history of mankind, and therefore the latest religion revealed has to be the most hard and exoteric in order to hold the masses, which means that its higher implications will be veiled in the most cryptic and symbolical form. That is the case with Islam.

But how does belief in the existence of Sufism from the very origin of Islam, in fact as the very essence of Islam, fit in with the evidence which historians and philosophers profess to find of its gradual development and of the influence on it of neo-Platonism? There is no doubt that neo-Platonism did exert an enormous influence on the formulation of Sufi philosophy. Modern philosophers could, therefore, hardly help regarding Sufi philosophy as a derivative of neo-Platonism once they made the initial error of considering it a philosophy at all. Of course it is not; it is a path, which is something quite different. Some of

Arthur Osborne 61

those who teach or follow a path may like to give a philosophical exposition of it, but there is no necessity to do so. Studying a philosophy is quite a different type of activity from following a path. Those philosophers who study neo-Platonic or Sufi philosophy today are not Sufis, are not even training to become Sufis, since they are not following a Sufi path, whereas I, on the other hand, when I set foot on the path, was not expected to study neo-Platonic or any other philosophy. No disciple of the Sufis is. A basic understanding of the theory of non-duality is expected, but that is simple; and after that practise, not theory, is needed.

Even if the philosophers had never formulated their theories at all, if there were no other texts, no books, no theories, the basic meaning is contained entire in the *shahada* itself: 'There is no god but God'; and according to Islamic tradition this has been used with full understanding, as a weapon for fighting the 'greater holy war', from the beginning. It is the same as that tremendous sentence from the *Bhagavad Gita:* "There is no existence of the unreal and no non-existence of the Real." Whether philosophers write books about it or not, whether they agree with Plato or not, does not concern the spiritual wayfarer, whose task is not to theorise about it but to use it.

I had not long returned to Bangkok before I received a letter from Martin saying that his guru had seen photographs of my *murshid* and some letters written by him and was not happy about him, in fact did not consider him a realized man. My wife had already formed such an opinion prior to this as soon as she heard my account of the guru and saw his picture. This started a general correspondence among those concerned that at times became acrimonious. My *murshid* revealed a talent for abuse that embarrassed me. Two more members of our original Guenon group were able to come to India despite the war; they met him and were not impressed. Martin wrote reminding me of Guenon's teaching that there were two grades of initiatic organization: that where the guru had only 'horizontal authenticity', that is to say valid appointment in succession to an unbroken chain of gurus, and that where he had 'vertical authenticity' also, that is direct connection, through realization, with the divine source of initiation. Initiation into the former should bestow a certain grace but could not lead to realization; for that the realized guru was necessary. This made a deep impression on me, for never at any time was I willing to relinquish pursuit of the Supreme Goal. I held out for a while, partly out of loyalty to my *murshid*, but largely also from reluctance to admit that I was in the wrong; but eventually I gave in, convinced of my error.

Years later I perceived how futile the whole dispute had been, when I appreciated at last the significance of the term 'Realized Man', and when I found that Martin's guru (whom I never met) was explaining that the guru need not be realized, while Martin himself was telling new aspirants that there was no hope of Realization in this lifetime. This is not mere pessimism but a sinking to the exoteric level. It betokens a failure of the basic understanding of non-duality required for the quest, and therefore, on the spiritual level, it is an error. It is itself an impediment to realization, since it vests the unreal with a temporary reality by asking when and whether it can cease to exist. Forgetting that 'there is no existence of the unreal and no non-existence of the Real', it substitutes the exoteric fallacy that there is a temporary existence of the unreal, which may be replaced by the Real on some future occasion. To put it quite simply, saying that you cannot attain Realization in this lifetime means asserting what you should deny — the existence of a 'you'

Arthur Osborne 63

who can or cannot attain — and thereby closes the door to Realization. The question whether you can attain or not ought not to arise; it ought to be dissolved in the real question: who is it that seeks to attain?

I did not grasp all this clearly at the time, but was quite determined not to remain on a path that did not lead to the Goal. Was there any benefit from the initiation I had rushed so impatiently to acquire and all the exercises I had done? Such a question is not always easy to answer. A man is ill, he takes medicine and gets better; but is it because of the medicine or in spite of it or independently of it? There seemed to be an increased depth and subtlety of understanding after the first initiation and of spiritual vigour after the second. It may be said that there was benefit from the determination and enthusiasm that made me seek.

So far as my *murshid* goes, I was never really wholehearted; perhaps that was what made it comparatively easy for me to abandon him. Others have been less fortunate, becoming attached to gurus who were not merely incomplete, lacking Self-realization (in that there is no harm so long as they recognize their limitation) but false and deluded, misguided and misguiding others. It is a sign of the times — the time of false Christs and false prophets of which Christ warned his followers. Some such are widely known and publicized, others almost unknown. They make the highest possible claims for themselves, or allow their disciples to make them: this one is Christ at his second coming, that one is God Incarnate. How far they are self-deluded and how far consciously deluding others is usually very hard to say. A man may spend years in solitude, practising yogic discipline, as a result of which various powers may develop, both internal powers such as vision and audition, and outward directed powers such as telepathy and

64 *My Life and Quest*

hypnotism. Then the ego, forgetting that its own immolation is the ultimate goal of the process, may pride itself on what it has acquired, regarding this as realization. In some cases this capital, accumulated during the time of training, may be gradually exhausted, like an overdrawn bank account, and the guru survives on his former reputation, if at all; but in other cases it may continue or even grow with the growth of the ego. For the ego will grow; there is no food on which it flourishes more than the adulation of disciples. The seeker needs to use great caution in estimating not only the guru but also the purity of his own motives, for any impure motive may be reflected outwardly in an imperfect guide. And then not only will he not be led forward into greater purity but will be infected by the imperfections of the guide, drifting into a worse state than before; for qualities of the ego are as infectious through psychic contact as a disease is through the physical.

Some time during my stay at Bangkok I stopped reading. I had read voraciously ever since first discovering Guenon; but the time came when I felt: "I know the theory now; it is practise that is needed." It was not just an option but also something deeper. I felt an actual aversion to the books which had so attracted me. This was a sound intuition. In almost all cases some doctrinal understanding is necessary at the beginning, and this needs to be more or less elaborate according to the temperament of the seeker and the nature of the path followed. From the beginning I was drawn to the direct path, which I will describe in a later chapter. Because this is known as *Jnana Marga* or Path of Knowledge, some have supposed it to be more theoretical than other paths, but the opposite is true. What is meant by 'Knowledge' is not learning but direct intuitional understanding. In fact, the more direct a path is the less theory it

Arthur Osborne 65

requires; it is the indirect paths, such as hermeticism and tantrism, that are based on elaborate theory.

In any case, whatever the path followed, there is no benefit from learning and re-learning once the mind is convinced. Not only does it not help, but also it is one of the ways in which the aspirant can be sidetracked, turning away from spiritual effort to the easier alternative of mental exertion. Not only individual seekers but communities also deteriorate in this way. Often the followers of unscholarly ecstatics become scholars, but it marks a spiritual decline. This is a mode of decline that is apt to be found in all religions — from the saint to the scholar.

Apart from providing an easy alternative to spiritual effort, excessive study can actually do positive harm by breeding pride in one's learning. I have even seen people reading to enjoy the self-satisfaction of feeling that they understood better than the writer.

The Maharshi was immensely learned but he became so unintentionally and without valuing learning. Devotees brought him books to read so that he could expound them, and his memory was such that he retained whatever he read. But he warned against barren erudition.

> "What use is the learning of those who do not seek to wipe out the letters of destiny (from their brow) by enquiry 'Whence is the birth of us who know the letters?' They have sunk to the level of a gramophone. What else are they, O' Arunachala?

> "It is those who are not learned who are saved rather than those whose ego has not yet subsided in spite of their learning. The unlearned are saved from the relentless grip of self-infatuation; they are saved from the malady of a myriad whirling thoughts and words; they are saved

from running after (mental) wealth. It is from more than one evil that they are saved."

— *The Collected Works of Ramana Maharshi*

By the 'unlearned' he means, of course, the simple-minded, not merely the ignorant, and by 'the learned' those who value and accumulate learning, not all who possess it.

For some years after this I scarcely read a book. To read books of no spiritual value — travel, fiction, politics and so forth — would have been even more a turning aside from the quest, degrading it to the level of a hobby or a part-time activity or an activity among others, one aspect of life, instead of the goal and the purpose of life. Therefore I did not read at all. Does this mean that I was a fanatic? No more than a man climbing Everest is a fanatic for not indulging in violin practise at the same time. I was one-pointed, not fanatical — and not one-pointed enough or the progress would have been greater. I never objected to reading in principle or tried to persuade others not to read; but I had an objective in life and did not want to distract my mind from it. The question has often been asked why men want to climb Everest, reach the North Pole, descend to the ocean's depths, tread the face of the moon, or in general attain the almost unattainable, and why they undergo all manner of hardships and face death in the attempt. The true answer is that all such cravings are blind physical reflections of man's innate urge to undertake the supreme quest for his lost homeland, for the utter freedom and perfect bliss of his true state. That is the real adventure, the well-neigh impassable road to the unattainable goal. The least the adventurer who dares attempt it can do is to be one-pointed in his enterprise. It is no idle ramble.

When I started reading again it was a different way and for a different reason, as I shall explain later.

Arthur Osborne 67

Early in 1941 my original contract with the Siamese (by now renamed 'Thai') government lapsed and was replaced by a permanent one. Between the two I became eligible for six months home leave. If it had not been for the war we should probably have gone far enough West to seek initiation from Martin's guru, but under the circumstances this was impossible. It also proved unnecessary, because Martin wrote that his guru now had a delegate in India who was authorised to give initiation in his name.

We had heard of the Maharshi by this time and had received some of his writings and some photographs of him, which made a tremendous impression on us. However, one of our original Guenon group had been to Tiruvannamalai to investigate and had reported that the Maharshi was not a guru and did not give initiation or spiritual guidance. This report had been relayed to us and it made it seem not worthwhile going there. Of this more later.

We were travelling now as a family of five. We spent some time in Rawalpindi where we enjoyed the keen, invigorating air and the scent of pine-trees, then up to Murree, a beautiful hill station, then on to Kashmir to meet the delegate. I was afraid to take a houseboat, as most visitors to Srinagar do, because the children were small and the two eldest like quicksilver, and we should have been constantly anxious that they would fall into the water. However, we were fortunate enough to get a rambling old house with a large garden stretching right down to the shore of one of the lakes. It was a delightful holiday. When we arrived there were wild irises by the roadside and luscious red cherries in the shops. One kind of fruit and flowers succeeded another through the summer. The two eldest children were at a delightful age — Catherine five and Adam two — only Frania was still too young to be very interesting. Catherine was as intelligent as she was lovely. Strangers would stop to ask who she was. When I tried to put her off by telling her that I would explain something when she was older, she would say: "All right, Daddy, but try now, and if I don't understand I'll tell you". She usually did understand. Adam was still enjoying the adventure of walking and talking.

There was no question this time of recognising a spiritual master because the delegate was not even supposed to be such. Some spiritual force seemed to be transmitted. There seemed to be an increase of vigour and power, as with the previous initiation there had been of subtlety.

9

Tribulation

IN SEPTEMBER 1942 our long and beautiful Kashmir holiday came to an end. But where next? The Japanese had already occupied French Indo-China (as it then was) and were adopting a belligerent tone. Thailand might well be the next on their list. The Consulate had asked British civilians in Thailand to stay at their posts as a means of maintaining some influence there, and in fact had let it be known that they would be turned down if they enlisted. And in any case the life I was leading there seemed more in accordance with my nature, and therefore more conducive to the quest, than campaigning. It was decided that I should go back while my wife stayed on in India with the three children.

But where? She was between two worlds. She had also received initiation, but she was certainly not quite convinced about the path we adopted; and followed it more for my sake than her own.

Once in Bangkok we had seen an exquisite little stone figure of the Buddha sitting cross-legged with the *naga,* the seven-

70 *My Life and Quest*

headed serpent, reared over him to give him shade; a figure of rare serenity. The price was very high or so it seemed to us, so my wife persuaded the shopkeeper to lend us it for a week so that she could obtain some clay through our neighbour, an Italian professor of sculpture, and set to work. What she produced was far from the original, but it was nevertheless an impressive piece of work. Being caught by the love of sculpture, she made next a bust of me. This was really excellent, so we had a bronze cast of it made. Shortly before she was due to leave Thailand we received some photographs of the Maharshi and (here is the point of this digression) my wife immediately felt the impulse to make a sculpture of him. Perhaps this was the deciding consideration, because she was still far from certain how far the quest was genuine and how far it was all play-acting.

One of our original Guenon group had a house at Tiruvannamalai and when he invited her to spend the time of our separation there, she immediately thought of the sculpture and it seemed the perfect solution. Even socially it seemed ideal, the people there being neither modern in the sense of superficial nor traditional in the sense of obscurantist.

We parted at Lahore railway station, my wife and children going on to Bombay and the south, I to Calcutta and Thailand. I spent my 35th birthday in Calcutta on my outward journey; I was to spend my 39th birthday there on the way back before I saw my wife or children again.

Catherine was the first to see Bhagavan. She stepped into the hall where he used to sit, a small, beautiful child with curly gold hair, bearing a tray of fruit in her hands, the customary offering. Bhagavan pointed to the low table beside his couch where such offerings were placed, and she, misunderstanding, sat down on it herself, holding the tray in her lap. There was a

Arthur Osborne 71

burst of laughter. "She has given herself as an offering to Bhagavan," someone said.

A day or two later my wife entered the hall and sat down. Immediately Bhagavan turned his luminous eyes on her in a gaze so concentrated that there was a vibration she could actually hear. She returned the gaze, losing all sense of time, the mind stilled, feeling like a bird caught by a snake, yet glad to be caught. An older devotee who watched told her that this was the silent initiation and that it had lasted about fifteen minutes. Usually it was quite short, a minute or two. She wrote to me that all her doubts had vanished; her objections no longer mattered. The idea of making a sculpture had been put aside; it seemed presumptuous. She had complete faith. She knew now that the teaching was true and that nothing else mattered. The most beautiful face, she told me, looked commonplace beside him, even though his features were not good. His eyes had the innocence of a small child, together with unfathomable wisdom and immense love.

For her this was the time of grace and wonder, as the first reading of Guenon had been for me, only far more vivid, having the living Master before her. She felt his power and guidance constantly. During the years of our separation — most of those four years with no news of one another — she did not worry, although by temperament prone to worrying. When offered a job she did not accept it, although by nature provident. The time to go out into the world would come later; this was the time to be with Bhagavan. Once, when she wanted to take leave of him before taking the children to the hills for the hot weather, she met him alone as he was returning from his daily walk on Arunachala and said to him: "Bhagavan, I understand that all I have to do is to keep quiet

72   *My Life and Quest*

and everything will be alright". And he confirmed it, his eyes
shining with approval.

He has been known to say: "Only keep quiet and I will do
the rest". But how hard it is to keep the mind quiet!

He was very gracious during these years both to her and
the children. They would come and show him their toys and
tell their secrets. At one of the big annual festivals his couch was
roped round with a sort of fence to keep the crowds from pressing
too close, and Adam scrambled through to tell him something.
He laughed and said to the attendants: "See how much use your
fence is!" In general he avoided touching people or being touched
by them, but each cool season when my wife brought the children
back from the hills, he touched Frania the youngest at some
time or other, and once he picked her up and carried her. He
was always very gracious to her.

My wife was receptive also to the spiritual power of
Arunachala. Before even she knew that it was a sacred
mountain, she dreamed one night of a terrific storm, when
the thunder crashed overhead, the wind uprooted ancient trees
and the rain beat down on the roof, that opened and revealed
a majestic figure, its personification, who summoned her
imperiously to the hill. Almost daily she walked there, feeling
its power of love and protection. Much of her meditation she
did on the hill. Lying on a sun-warmed rock one evening, she
had a vision of the whole world with its cities and men drawn
into her mouth as she inhaled.

The Japanese entered Thailand on December 8th, 1941.
After a few minutes token resistance the Thais surrendered and
became their allies. As I afterwards learned, they had previously
asked for help from Singapore but had been told that they would
have to help themselves. I think it was on December 7th that

Arthur Osborne 73

the Consulate sent word around advising us to leave the country; certainly it was too late to do so. The few who tried were turned back before they reached the frontiers. Moreover, the banks were closed so that it was impossible to draw out money.

In order to save the expenditure of manpower in creating a civilian administration and of the troops in holding down a conquered country, the Japanese decided to treat Thailand as a self-governing ally, and as a result their troops kept strict discipline and there were no atrocities, as there were in China and Malaya. I took a cycle rickshaw and went to the university, but there were Japanese officers and troops all over the place. In the university grounds I saw some officers with no trousers on, standing fishing in the *klongs*, the canals that run everywhere alongside the roads in Bangkok. It was impossible to resume duty, so I came back. After a day or two Europeans were placed under house arrest. Gradually they were rounded up and taken to an internment camp. My turn did not come till January 11th, one of the last. It was about time, because my salary had not been paid and I could not get out to cash a cheque.

While communications were still open I had received a letter from my wife telling me that Catherine and Adam had gone to Bhagavan and asked him to bring me back safely and he had smiled and nodded. From then on I never doubted that I should come out of it alive. There was also a letter from Catherine, one of the most moving I have ever received: "Daddy, you will love Bhagavan. When he smiles everybody must be so happy."

We were interned in the premises of the University of Political and Moral Sciences (not that in which I had taught). There were several long buildings on the bank of the river, a field big enough to play basketball, a gravel road running the

74   *My Life and Quest*

length of the camp. Some of the buildings were partitioned off into cubicles where the married couples and a few other fortunate ones enjoyed at least visual privacy, although every sound could be overheard; most of us had beds in common dormitories, with a little floor space each, which we fenced off as best we could with our belongings. There was a large shed at the back where we set up stoves and did a little private cooking, although our regular meals were sent in; also a shop where various articles from town made their appearance or could be ordered. After some time cash allowances began to be received through the Swiss consul. We were allowed to elect a camp committee and president to control the internal running of the camp. At first we were badly over-crowded, but after some time the Americans and Dutch and a few others were evacuated, and we ended up with not much more than a hundred.

The Thai, always keeping in mind that our side might win the war and hold them responsible, refused to make the camp over to the Japanese, so there were no atrocities. Indeed, one of the main evils to contend with was boredom. Any one who knew anything that others didn't started classes; books were circulated; amateur gardeners took over plots around the various buildings and made ornamental gardens. Towards the end, when victory and evacuation were visibly approaching, my garden became an excellent symbol to me of life in the world — I gave it daily care and had real interest in bringing it to perfection, while at the same time prepared to leave it at a moment's notice.

We knew well enough that victory was approaching because a small group of internees had taken the risk of smuggling in a wireless set and were skilful enough to keep it from the notice not only of the authorities but the rest of the internees also — unfortunately a necessary precaution. The news was leaked out so cleverly that we never knew from what source it came, only that it turned out to be reliable.

There were occasional Japanese inspections but the Thai commandant always warned us beforehand, so that anything that might cause trouble or be considered insufficiently austere might be concealed or passed out of the camp. The Thai soon had no more love for the Japanese than we had. Even though there were few outrages, their arrogance was insufferable.

The Thai had the bright idea of keeping their one and only submarine safe by anchoring it alongside our camp. Directly opposite us, on the banks of the river, were railway marshalling yards with stocks of rice, rubber and various other commodities, and it was hoped that our presence would safeguard them also; but it didn't work out that way.

Thailand had been forced to declare war on Britain and America and a florid announcement was made that the Allied bases had been pushed too far back to be able to bomb Bangkok. For quite a while it was so, and then the tide turned and fleets of American Fortresses began coming over, by night at first and then by day also, when the Japanese fighters no longer dared to go up during a raid. Whether SEATO headquarters knew about our camp or not, they certainly knew about the submarine and marshalling yards. A number of times they came over and set the whole of the opposite bank aflame with incendiaries. The submarine was not hit, but after one or two near misses, it sought shelter elsewhere. After bombing the opposite bank the huge Fortresses would zoom up over our camp, so low that they seemed to be skimming the roofs, their under-bellies glowing red from the reflected flames. Several times, when smoke blanketed the river, bombs dropped on our side also. We heard their deep, heavy thud around us. In the daytime we would see them actually

76   *My Life and Quest*

leaving the planes and swooping down — always on a trajectory. Twice, bombs fell within the camp precincts, but I was not the only one who preferred the risk of bombs to that of snakes and scorpions. There were many who never went underground. The flimsy modern buildings, with ample door and window space, stood up to the blasts better than more solid structures might have done.

I neither gave nor attended any of the numerous classes, but it was in camp that I learned astrology. One of the internees, Leslie, was a lifelong addict and brought a whole trunk full of books in with him — all of Alan Leo and Carter and a number of other books, including a good one on the progressed horoscope, besides bound volumes of periodicals. Making a purposeful break in my non-reading epoch, I went steadily through them, studying and making notes. This took me some months, after which I reverted to my non-reading. There were books circulating in camp, but I did not borrow or read them. Leslie's interest had remained mainly theoretical; he had very seldom actually attempted a horoscope. I, of course, wanted to practise, and under my influence he also began to. We made horoscopes for everyone who wanted them in camp; and a number of internees, pleased with the product, asked for them also for wives or children or others outside.

Many people dismiss astrology in the same doctrinaire attitude of mind in which Guenon dismissed Buddhism. If they were to read through a study in several pages of some person the astrologer did not know, giving his characteristics and aptitudes and the main lines of his destiny, they would see that it could not be lucky guesswork, just as Guenon would have seen, if he had studied Buddhist texts, that they could not be giving the true teaching by accident; but they are unwilling even to consider

Arthur Osborne 77

the evidence, so convinced are they *a priori* that the movements of planets in the heavens cannot influence the lives of men on earth. Actually, it would be rather a crude definition of astrology which said that they could; the real interpretation is more vast and more profound: that the entire universe is one tremendous harmony, that the same forces are at work in the macrocosm and the microcosm, the cosmos and the individual, that the tendencies in a man and the events in his life flow to the same rhythm as the planetary movements in the skies; that, although the intricacy of the arrangement would make a mathematician's mind reel, no individual can be born except at the moment when the position of the heavens is such as to mirror his nature and destiny.

It is a typical misunderstanding which led some people in camp to argue that a man's character is not formed by the positions of the stars at his birth but by heredity. Actually, it is never said that the positions of the stars form a man's character but that they indicate it; and heredity is one of the influences which they indicate. It often happens that several members of a family are born at about the same time of day or have birthdays at about the same date, and both of these are varieties of family likeness which would show in a horoscope, though, of course, by no means the only ones.

Leslie and I had an interesting case of family likeness showing in horoscopes. There were two brothers in camp, middle-aged, whose families were outside — evacuated while there was still time. One of them asked me to do his horoscope and the other Leslie. Satisfied with his own, the one who had asked me then asked me to do that of his ten-year-old son, whom I had never seen. I was struck by the fact (although I did not tell him so) that the boy's horoscope showed no likeness to his own.

Some days later I saw Leslie working on a horoscope which at once struck me as showing a distinct family likeness to that of the boy. Intrigued, I asked him whose it was, and he told me that it was that of the daughter of the other brother and that it showed no similarity to her father's. I may say that the two brothers themselves were noticeably alike. I then went to them and told them that their two children seemed to have a strong family likeness but not to take after them. "Yes," they said, "both of them take after our mother, but we don't."

When I said that Leslie had previously confined himself mainly to theory, I meant the theory of applied astrology, but there is also a more profound type of theory, the divine or spiritual cosmology writ in the symbols of the stars. Jupiter and Saturn, for example, are the twin forces of expansion and contraction — creation and dissolution of the universe, the day and night of God, the breathing out and in of Brahma. In human life they may show as prosperity and adversity, indulgence and discipline, in caricature as Sir Toby Belch and Malvolio; and on the quest they are the complementary process of expansion and contraction to which I referred in an earlier chapter. I worked out this more essential theory partly from study and partly from my previous knowledge of spiritual cosmology and wrote a book on it which I called *The Cosmology of the Stars.*

After leaving camp and coming to Bhagavan I gave up astrology. I was not sorry to have learned it, but cosmological theory is unnecessary on the direct path, which I was now following, and there was no point in occupying my mind with it. It can, of course, be not merely unnecessary but harmful if one gets too engrossed in it. I have known more than one Hindu (and Hindu astrology concerns itself more with predictions than Western astrology does nowadays) who has dropped it because

Arthur Osborne 79

it was too accurate. Foreknowledge of misfortunes awaiting persons who consulted them caused them so much distress as to destroy their peace of mind.

To return to the level of applied astrology: I have nothing against Uranus; indeed he can be a very useful ingredient in a horoscope; but they do say that when in conjunction with the Moon he is liable to push even an intelligent person into occasional acts of unpredictable folly. I have recorded two such already. The first, my throwing away the chance of an Oxford career, concealed an underlying wisdom; it was not foolish in itself but only in the way it was carried out. The second, my profession of Islam, was foolish both in itself and in the way it was done; nevertheless even here there was some underlying grace in it and, if unnecessary at the time, it was soon to become necessary according to the code by which I was living. At the time of my arrest Uranus scored a third victory, this time with an act of pure unmitigated folly with no grace or wisdom in it at all. I came into camp wearing a turban and long gown and with a string of prayer beads round my neck.

It was not exhibitionism. Indeed I simply estimated that the internment would not last for more than about three months and decided to devote the time entirely to prayer, meditation, incantations and reading the Arabic *Quran* and to hold completely aloof from the profane crowd in the camp; and I dressed to symbolise my decision. Also I am of a retiring disposition and prefer to remain inconspicuous. Actually the internment lasted for three and half years and I soon changed into normal clothing and, for the first time in my life, did mix with a crowd of ordinary, unpretentious people, and found that I liked them. This was a necessary phase in my development, making good what I had failed to do at Oxford, for my refusing

80   *My Life and Quest*

to mix there had been due only in part to disappointed idealism; partly also it was a mixture of timidity and conceit.

One of the things that struck me most powerfully was their fair-mindedness. I do not refer only to their acceptance of myself as soon as I was prepared to be accepted (though that might well be called magnanimous); but throughout the years of internment it happened a number of times that one person or another would make himself unpopular, and in every case I found that as soon as the cause of disapproval was removed, the camp as a whole spontaneously recognized the fact and, so to speak, welcomed him back into its fellowship. Of course, there were quarrels; it was a very average community and I do not want to make it appear in any way ideal. Some of the women took advantage of being in a minority; also there was tension among the camp politicians who aspired to get elected to the committee and run things; but on the whole there was a good spirit.

Another thing that struck me was the prevailing dissatisfaction with life — and I do not mean conditions in camp but with life itself, as it had been outside before they were affected by the war. And these people were not misfits or failures. Most of them were at least averagely successful, with a good job, a wife and family, better pay than they would have received at home in England, comfortable house and servants, and a full social life; yet it was surprising how many would confide that life held no meaning for them and that, while outside, they had drunk heavily in order to forget and not to think.

It is dissatisfaction with the false that leads a man to seek the true. When asked why one should seek Self-realization, Bhagavan has been known to answer: "Who asked you to? If you are satisfied with your present life, stay as you are. But many

Arthur Osborne 81

people become dissatisfied, and when you realize the Self your discontent will vanish."

There were also more specific signs of discontent — three broken marriages, four cases of madness, one suicide. A very sociable, good-hearted man, a complete extrovert one would have said, borrowed Paul Brunton's *A Search in Secret India* from me in order to read about the Maharshi. On giving it back, he said: "Yes, well, when one reads about something like Ramana Maharshi one either does nothing about it — or else..." He seemed so unlikely to do anything about it that I said no more to him, nor he to me; but soon after the camp broke up, at the end of the war, I heard that he had committed suicide.

The most dynamic sign of discontent was that as many as seven of the internees joined me, pledging their lives to the quest, apart from a penumbra of others who sympathised without deciding to take the plunge.

However, before that happened I passed through a lengthy period of dryness and tribulation, a dark night of the soul when I knew the taste of tears, even though with no outer weeping. It no longer seemed a quest that I was making but a vast impersonal process that was taking place, hammering the living being into shape, and with no anaesthetic. Suffering seemed the very essence of life and 'pain-bearer' the definition of man. I was tempted to despond, to regard God as a tyrant Who torments His creatures.

There seemed no light, no grace, and no hope of progress; and yet to go back, to renounce the quest, was even more impossible; in fact the very idea never arose. I just clung on grimly, suffering. The outer conditions of life accorded well with the inner misery but did not cause it, any more than outer conditions cause the unspeakable bliss when grace floods the heart. Indeed, before I left the camp I was to know periods of

82   *My Life and Quest*

some grace also, though not at it's fullest. There was a lot in me that had to be burnt out, and this period of savage pain was largely due to the cauterisation. Even at the time I knew this, but that did not make me like it.

I did not proselytise. The love of argument was one of the things that had been burnt out of me. I preferred to avoid it as far as possible. I still do. Some approached me themselves; some persuaded each other. This, of course, was proselytism, even though I did not do it myself. Proselytism cannot always be condemned, although it is better to be chary of it. Spiritual understanding places an obligation on a man, and if he has not the endurance and integrity to take this up he is more culpable than before. That is the point of Christ's saying that it was not a sin to be in darkness when there was no light but only to cling to the darkness when light was made available. Therefore the reckless proselytiser may be doing a disservice to those to whom he speaks. That is why initiatic bodies have normally kept their teaching secret, and why Christ warned against casting pearls before swine. Incidentally, this is one of those sayings of Christ's which can have no possible meaning to those who have reduced Christianity to an exoteric shell. What are the pearls and who the swine? And what is there they need fear to reveal? All that they know they proclaim endlessly to whoever will listen. On the other hand, what wonder if those who seek the pearls of wisdom and are given only the exoteric shell find the religion they are taught unsatisfying?

Louis Hartz was one who approached me himself. A very conspicuous young man from Holland who, for some reason or other, had not been evacuated with the rest of the Dutch; short, with black hair and eager eyes, he was obviously seeking. Several times he engaged an associate of mine in long discussions but

Arthur Osborne 83

went away unconvinced. Then I saw him walking up and down the camp with an elderly gentleman who had at one time been the head of a school or college and overheard a snatch of their talk as they passed:

"When I was younger I read the Bible, but of course I don't believe it now."

"Well — er — Mr. Hartz, what exactly in the Bible do you not believe?"

"All of it."

In view of such a brash reply, it can be imagined that I was not disposed to explain to him at any great length, much less to enter into an argument, when he approached me a day or two later and announced that he wanted to know the Truth.

"I will tell you one truth," I said. "Infinity minus x is a contradiction in terms, because by the exclusion of x the first term ceases to be infinite."

Yes, he saw that.

"Very well, then," I told him, "think of Infinity as God and x as yourself. Now go and think it over and come tomorrow and tell me what you make of it."

That was all; no more explanation.

When he came back next day he told me that there had been no need to think it over. Before even he got back to his place in the dormitory it had flashed on his heart that it was true.

He had been ripe for understanding and therefore a single explanation had been enough. Moreover, it had been the right kind of explanation that I was led to give him, because, like my wife, he had the intuitive type of mind which cannot read a whole chapter about what can be said in a sentence. He could never read Guenon, but he read and re-read the *Tao Te Ching*.

84   *My Life and Quest*

However, brilliant initial understanding is no guarantee of a smooth or rapid quest. Since Realization is quite different from mental understanding, every preoccupation with the ego is an obstacle to progress on it. The process must continue until the whole nature is transmuted and all egoism dissolved.

The internees found various occupations during the daytime; in the evening many of them used to sit around on the lawn in small groups, and ours formed one group among the others. A certain power flowed through me at that time. Sometimes two of the group would discuss some point and decide to ask me about it in the evening, and when evening came I would spontaneously explain it without the question being raised. One person who joined us was of a psychic disposition, and the first time he sat in our evening group he saw a vortex of blue light encircling it and rising to a spiral in the centre. In general I had a feeling of how to respond to the needs of the various people, what to say and do.

This illustrates the dangers of a false guru. There is nothing personal in such powers. I had never consciously practised telepathy and I myself never saw any blue lights; even if I had it would have meant nothing; and yet on the basis of such happenings a man can build up a reputation for himself and start posing as a guru, and if he attributes the power to himself it will be both to his detriment and to that of the people he is supposed to be guiding.

Fortunately I was not drawn into any such aberration. Indeed, before the camp broke up I had ceased to exert any influence or to guide the others at all. There was a psychic crisis in camp when one went mad and most of those who had joined me took fright and drew back. That was what was visible outwardly, but inner events are more fundamental, and in myself

Arthur Osborne 85

I felt at this time a cessation of the power of guidance. I no longer felt that I knew what to do and say; I no longer felt any influence over the others; nor did they any longer feel it. This did not seem to me a privation or a cause for regret, simply a change of course, because the interest in guiding others evaporated together with the power to do so. I vaguely felt it to be a transfer from the spiritual influence of the order into which I had been initiated to that of Bhagavan. More and more I felt his presence and he seemed to dominate and to bestow grace. Although I had only seen him in photographs, his face was more vivid to me, more easily visualized, than any I had ever known. I was content simply to feel his pervading graciousness without occupying my mind at all with what I had been told about his not being a guru.

Bhagavan, as I was later to discover, did not encourage people to play the guru, even to the limited extent to which I had been doing so. He would not absolutely forbid it, for that would be doctrinaire. If asked he might say: "If it is a man's destiny to be a guru he will be." And he knew that some of his devotees acted so. But on the whole he discouraged it. Even apart from the direct and obvious danger of flattering a man's ego and perhaps inducing him to let himself be regarded as a realized man when he is not, it means a turning of the energy outwards when the aspirant still needs to turn it inwards. If it does not actually put a stop to his further progress, it at least makes it more difficult.

And what happened afterwards? Of all those I had known in camp only Hartz was drawn to Bhagavan after the war. For the first year or two he concentrated on building up a business and making money. Then he broke a business trip from Europe to Thailand to spend a few days at Tiruvannamalai. It was the hot season when I was in the hills with my family. The children were going to a convent school in the hills and we used to spend

86   My Life and Quest

several months there in the summer, so as to be able to take them out of the boarding house and have them at home with us. I went to Colombo to meet Hartz and we spent the night at the house of K. Ramachandra, a friend who always welcomed devotees of Bhagavan. Next day we flew to Madras and stayed with Dr. T.N. Krishnaswami, another devotee. The railway journey from there to Tiruvannamalai is roundabout and takes a whole day and night, and the excellent bus service which now plies had not yet been started, so Hartz hired a car for the trip. He was not averse to showing the advantages of being wealthy.

Bhagavan was very gracious to him. Indeed, a photograph of Bhagavan taken by him on this trip is evidence enough of the love and encouragement with which Bhagavan regarded him. He received the initiation by look, but, although told by the devotees that this was Bhagavan's mode of initiation, he wanted to make quite sure and therefore said: "I want Bhagavan's initiation." Bhagavan replies: "You have it already." This is the only occasion of which I know when he explicitly confirmed having given initiation.

In another way also Hartz desired assurance: he perhaps feared that when he got back into life of the world with all its distractions his steadfastness might weaken. He asked Bhagavan for some guarantee and was given the tremendous assurance: "Even if you let go of Bhagavan, Bhagavan will never let go of you."

Once Bhagavan has taken up a person, his destiny becomes more purposeful, is speeded up, so to say. From a worldly point of view this may be for good or ill; prosperity may be needed for one man's development, adversity for another. Evidently Hartz was of the latter type, because from this time his business got into difficulties and within a few years it had evaporated

Arthur Osborne 87

completely. He had planned to come back and even to build a house at Tiruvannamalai, but he was not able to. How many such cases have I seen, where the first visit was made easy but a planned return was frustrated year after year! He went through many vicissitudes and for a period of years I did not hear from him at all; but Bhagavan did not let go of him.

And the others? Perhaps some of them followed some other path, perhaps not. I have already indicated in an earlier chapter that what educationalists would call 'the percentage of wastage' is very high on the quest. Christ warned of this when he said that many are called but few are chosen — another of his sayings to which exoteric Christianity can give no meaning. Called to what and chosen for what? Certainly not to membership of a Christian church or it would be manifestly untrue. They take as many as they can get. Then for what? For heaven? That would carry with it the rather grim corollary that the great majority of mankind go to hell. But as soon as one understands the esoteric teaching of the quest, the saying becomes a statement of what happens and corresponds with what is taught in all religions. The *Bhagavad Gita* says the same, only expanding it to show that the not-called are even more numerous: "Among thousands, perhaps one strives for Realization; among thousands who strive for Realization, perhaps one knows Me as I am." (Ch. 7, v. 3).

It rests with the aspirant himself. No one can do the work for him. The Buddha's last words to his followers were an exhortation to strive and be a light for themselves and a haven for themselves. Sometimes a devotee would try to inveigle Bhagavan into a statement that his grace alone was sufficient without effort on the part of the devotee, but without success. He said once: "If the guru could just give Realization there would not be even a cow left unrealised." In the language of mediaeval mythology, the guru may give the magic sword and the cloak of invisibility, but it is the hero himself who must use them and achieve victory — or fail to do so. True, these people had not yet any guru; but at least they knew where to seek. When I first read Guenon I did not even know that. Whoever perseveres is guided somehow or other, although he may be sorely tried on the way.

10

BHAGAVAN SRI RAMANA MAHARSHI

The parts of this chapter about Bhagavan's teachings are largely based on The Teachings of Ramana Maharshi in His Own Words. *There are also quotations from* Ramana Arunachala.

I FOUND MY wife changed when I met her at Tiruvannamalai after four years. She had been mature in character before but now she was mature in understanding also. She no longer asked for explanations but gave them. And as she was explaining the same truths in a different idiom, that of Bhagavan instead of that of Guenon, it took me some time to adjust myself.

Bhagavan did not immediately reveal himself to me. I felt far less from his bodily presence than I had from his invisible support in camp. His photograph had been more real and vivid to me than any person, and yet now that I saw him face-to-face I felt his presence much less. This did not unduly worry me; it seemed merely a confirmation of what I had been told, that he was not a guru. I will give my impressions as I wrote them down at a time when they were fresher in my mind.

"I entered the ashram hall on the morning of my arrival, before Bhagavan had returned from his daily walk on the hill. I was a little awed to find how small it was and how close to him I should be sitting; I had expected something grander and less intimate. And then he entered and, to my surprise, there was no great impression. Certainly far less than his photograph had made. Just a white-haired, very gracious man, walking a little stiffly from rheumatism and with a slight stoop. As soon as he had eased himself on to the couch he smiled at me and then turned to those around and to my young son and said: 'So Adam's prayer has been answered; his Daddy has come back safely.' I felt his kindness but no more. I appreciated that it was for my sake that he had spoken English, since Adam knew Tamil."

The change came a few weeks later at one of the big festivals of the ashram year. "There were huge crowds for the festival and we were sitting in the courtyard outside the hall. Bhagavan was reclining on his couch and I was sitting in the front row before it. He sat up, facing me, and his narrowed eyes pierced into me, penetrating, intimate, with an intensity I cannot describe. It was as though they said: 'You have been told; why have you not realized?' And then quietness, a depth of peace, an indescribable lightness and happiness.

"Thereafter love for Bhagavan began to grow in my heart and I felt his power and beauty. Next morning, for the first time, sitting before him in the hall, I tried to follow his teaching by using the *vichara*, 'Who am I?'. I thought it was I who had decided. I did not at first realize that it was the initiation by look that had vitalized me and changed my attitude of mind. Indeed, I had only heard vaguely of this initiation and paid little heed to what I had heard. Only later did I learn that other

Arthur Osborne 91

devotees also had had such an experience, and that with them also it had marked the beginning of active *sadhana* (quest) under Bhagavan's guidance."

Then, for the first time in my life, I began to understand what the grace and blessing of the guru could mean. "My love and devotion to Bhagavan deepened. I went about with a lilt of happiness in my heart, feeling the blessing and mystery of the guru, repeating, like a song of love, that he was the Guru, the link between heaven and earth, between God and me, between the Formless Being and my heart. I became aware of the enormous grace of his presence. Even outwardly he was gracious to me, smiling when I entered the hall, signing to me to sit where he could watch me in meditation."

However, with the Sadguru, the Divine Guru, this simple, idyllic state could not long continue. Although the devotion never diminished, it had merged with understanding. "And then one day a vivid reminder awoke in me: 'The link with Formless Being? But he is the Formless Being.' And I began to apprehend the meaning of his *Jnana* and to understand why devotees addressed him simply as 'Bhagavan', which is a name for God. (I should have said: 'A word meaning God'). So he began to prove in me what he declared in his teaching: that the outer guru serves to awaken the guru in the heart. The *vichara*, the constant 'Who am I?' began to awaken an awareness of the Self as Bhagavan outwardly and also simultaneously of the Self within.

The specious theory that Bhagavan was not a Guru had simply evaporated in the radiance of his Grace. Moreover, I now perceived that, far from his teaching not being practical guidance, it was exclusively that. I observed that he shunned theoretical explanations and kept turning the questioner to practical considerations of *sadhana*, of the path to be followed. It was that and only that he was here to teach!

Before going any further I will try briefly to elucidate the differences of meaning in the terms 'saint', 'mystic', 'initiate', 'yogi', and 'sage'. It will help to show what we implied by using the term 'Bhagavan' and what Bhagavan prescribed and therefore will not really be a digression. These terms, of course, are not rigorously precise definitions; neither are they mutually exclusive; nevertheless they do indicate real differences, even though there may be overlapping.

Imagine people living in a miasma at the foot of a mountain, stunted, undernourished, wasted by disease. They have been told that there is a wonderful plateau on the mountaintop, with fruit and flowers, invigorating air and cool, fresh water. But the ascent is arduous and they would have to leave their hovels and their few miserable possessions behind, so they stay where they are. Only a few of the more enterprising, either seeking the mountain summit or simply striving to rise above the heat, miasma and mosquitoes of the plain, have climbed up some distance and made themselves dwellings on the hillside. The plain-dwellers would refer to them all alike as 'people of the hill' and yet there would be endless differences among them. Some might have developed a farmstead and have fruit, milk and grain to give away to the sick and needy below, while others might be resting in a cave with a little more than their immediate needs. Some might have set forth on a deliberate enterprise to attain the summit, while others were driven merely by the urge to get up higher into cooler air and more beautiful, health-giving surroundings, not even knowing that there was a summit to attain. Even among those who started out with a plan of ascent, some might have put it aside till a later, indefinite

Arthur Osborne 93

date, once they had made a home somewhere along the path, while others might regard each pleasure-grove they came to as no more than a resting place from which to plan the next stage of the ascent.

No less varied are the people known as 'saints'. Not only in their level of attainment do they vary but in their understanding of the goal and their dedication to further striving towards it. Also in the powers they manifest and the benefits they bestow. Only the Roman Catholic Church officially canonises saints; in other religions they are simply recognized. One criterion the Church demands is the performance of miracles. Power may flow through a saint, but it is by no means necessary that he should be interested to manifest powers. Also, the possession of powers is no proof of sainthood. This the Church recognizes. Not only that, but Christ himself warned against false prophets who would perform signs and wonders.

The mention of powers invites consideration of a slightly different category, that of the yogi or initiate (for the yogi is simply an initiate of one particular type of Hindu path). There is no clear demarcation; indeed, a saint may be a member of an initiatic order, while an initiate who has attained to a higher state will be a saint. Nevertheless, the accent here is rather more on powers and faculties and less on sanctity. The initiate is following a definite technique intended to cause changes and development of mind and character and ultimately to lead to beatitude; the saint also may be, but he may have been swept up by the sheer force of his aspiration and devotion, not knowing in theory whither he is being borne or by what means. There were initiatic sciences (hermetic or alchemical) in mediaeval Christendom and still are in India (yogic and tantric sciences) which develop powers and faculties in a man such as would be generally termed supernatural.

94 *My Life and Quest*

Purity of character and motive are supposed to be essential in these sciences, but unfortunately there are people who practise them without and become rather occultists than saints. I myself have seen people in India who could perform wonders, and there was nothing spiritual about them. The great Tibetan Buddhist saint Milarepa (whose life has been translated into English by Evans-Wentz) first attained occult powers for the egoistic purpose of revenge on relatives who had dispossessed his mother and himself; when he turned to a genuine spiritual path he had to undergo terrible austerities to purify himself from this aberration. The meaning of 'initiate', therefore, ranges all the way from 'saint' on the one hand to 'occultist' on the other, apart from the many initiates, indeed the great majority, who achieve no recognizable development at all as a result of their initiation.

The term 'mystic' also is vaguely used. Both a saint and the initiate may be a mystic — in fact it might be held that the genuine saint and the successful initiate must be. However, there can be mystics who are neither saints nor initiates. The emphasis here is rather on intuitive knowledge, vision or ecstasy than on either sanctity or powers. Moreover, it may be a passive state without either the theoretical understanding or the practical disciplines of the initiate and without the saint's striving for purity. What is held to characterise it is the occasional largesse of vision or beatitude, descending unearned. Even here there is a very wide range of what the mystic glimpses, from pure Self-realization to sensual visions and divine visitations.

There is one flank of the mountain where the ascent is sheer, with no pleasant groves to rest in on the way, where, to compensate for this, the path is direct and the crest already visible from the plains below and throughout the ascent. This is the direct path taught by Bhagavan. There are no stages on this path. Indeed, followers of Bhagavan are apt to be impatient when they hear of stages or degrees of realization upon some indirect path and to say: 'What does all this mean? Either a man has realized the Self or he has not.' This attitude is right as regards their own path but not necessarily as regards others, for there are paths on which the wayfarer does not aim at realization of the Self, the ultimate end of Supreme Truth, or at any rate not directly, and the term 'realization' is used with a different meaning, to signify merely the attainment of some higher state which, however, is equally transient and illusory within the ultimate reality of the Self.

However, although the wayfarer on the direct path does not attain to any higher states along the way, he may be blessed with glimpses of pure Self-realization, beyond all states, which will suffuse and irradiate his whole life. Speaking of pure Self-realization and the direct path to it, Bhagavan affirmed quite definitely both, that there are no stages in Realization and that Realization is not normally permanent when first attained. It may come in occasional flashes but cannot be permanent until the *vasanas* (inherent tendencies impelling one to desire one thing and shun another) have been eradicated.

Two modes of conscious planned ascent have now been indicated, whatever name one may give them (apart from the occasional transportation of the mystic and the uncharted elevation of certain saints): that of the man who ascends in stages, becoming stabilized in this lifetime in some higher state, possibly with higher powers, but with no direct, and often even no theoretical knowledge of the supreme state of Self-realization, and that of the man who envisages the supreme truth of Identity, strives towards it, perhaps has occasional glimpses of its Realization but, until attaining it, is not established in any higher state. Which is preferable? The question is unrealistic, since each aspirant will follow the path that accords with his temperament and that his destiny makes available.

Another question that may be raised at this point is that of the benefit to those below. Reverting to the symbol of the mountain: should the hill-dweller who is facing downwards, having established a homestead not too high up from which he can supply the sufferers in the plains below, not be considered preferable to one who has turned his back on them and struggled up on his lone path to the summit? He might be if the symbol held good, but it does not. It is cancelled out by Christ's saying that to him who attains the kingdom of heaven all else is added. It is therefore he who has greatest power to help others. One's own Self-realization is the greatest boon that one can bestow on others, while at the same time, paradoxically, it reveals that there are no others to whom to bestow boons. It is like waking up from a dream; and to ask what can be done for others is as senseless as worrying what happened to the people one saw in last night's dream. And yet waking is the best way to help them. Both are true.

Plontinus is usually spoken of as a sage and Eckhart as a mystic, and yet they would both appear to fall into the same category of wayfarers on the direct path. In theory they both showed complete understanding of the absolute Oneness of Self-realization, of what Guenon called the 'Supreme Identity'; in practise also they both seem to have had glimpses of realization such as Bhagavan refers to, although it is clear from what they themselves wrote that they were not permanently and irrevocably in the state.

To be thus established is possible although very rare. Again, "Among thousands, perhaps one strives for realization; among thousands who strive for Realization, perhaps one knows Me as I am." (*Bhagavad Gita*, Ch. 7, verse 3). This does not imply knowing as one does another but knowing by being. It means simply to realize the Self that you always were by complete dissolution of any other-than-Self in you, or, more correctly still, by complete dissolution of the mistaken belief that there ever was any other-than-Self in you.

This is the supreme state. It is beyond revelation, for who is to reveal to whom? Beyond prayer, for who is to pray to whom? However, the realized man may consciously act a part on the stage of life where prayer, like any other activity, is to be performed. He may act any part in life — that of king or hermit, married or celibate, famous or obscure, according to his apparent nature and destiny. I say 'apparent' because in fact he has transcended nature and destiny.

Such a one was the Bhagavan I knew. He was the most simple, natural, unassuming of men; he was what a man should be, quite without affectation, like a child; and at the same time with an indescribable beauty and wisdom and with such power that many trembled in his presence and feared to speak to him. To address him in the third person, as 'Bhagavan', seemed less inappropriate than saying 'you' to one who was leading us beyond the duality of 'you' and 'I'. When the meaning was general and warranted it, he would also say 'Bhagavan' — "even if you let go of Bhagavan, Bhagavan will never let go of you". In simple daily affairs he would play the part of an individual, just as an actor could play Lear's frenzy without himself being frenzied, without supposing that he was Lear.

Unfortunately, few in the West understand the possibility of this supreme state. To make matters worse, the philosophers and theologians, who should be the ones to explain it, introduce

98   *My Life and Quest*

confusion by misunderstanding and therefore denying or misrepresenting it. In the East there is the opposite trouble—that this possibility is widely understood and is therefore claimed indiscriminately for every one who can gather disciples.

Bhagavan was also commonly referred to as 'the Maharshi' or 'Ramana Maharshi'. A pundit once explained to me that this title, condensed from 'Maha-Rishi', 'Great Sage', is applied to one who does not merely continue a tradition but inaugurates a new spiritual path. Certainly that would justify its application to Ramana Maharshi.

In speaking of spiritual men, the question also arises of their recognition. It is not uncommon to hear some one express confidence that he would recognise a spiritual man if he met one. This, however, is not always possible. High spiritual attainment, even complete liberation, is not always recognisable. Naturally, it is not easy to give examples of this, for this very reason that they are not recognised, but one very striking one is that of Christ before he set forth on his mission. According to Christian doctrine, he was born without original sin (which means Self-realization from birth) and attained no new state when he went forth on his 'Father's business'; and yet he exerted no influence on others before that but went completely unrecognised. Not only is there no record of crowds flocking to Nazareth, as they would have in any country or age to the seat of one recognized as a holy man, but, on the contrary, when he returned there with his disciples his fellow-townsmen expressed surprise, if not incredulity that the local carpenter should have turned out a prophet. The Maharshi also was not recognized when he first attained Realization but only later when he began to shed Grace on others and act as a Guru.

The reason for this is that it is not a man's inner state which is felt by others but the Grace flowing through him towards

Arthur Osborne 99

them. Perceptible Grace may thus flow through one who has not attained the Supreme Identity (as has been the case with many saints) or even through one who has not attained any spiritual state at all; and again it may not through one who has. There may be other spiritual functions besides the guidance of disciples, for some of which anonymity is desirable. If so it will be maintained.

With a guru, of course, the question of recognition ought not to arise, since it is, so to speak, his function to be recognized. It is important that he should be, because my saying that perceptible grace can flow through one who has not attained does not mean that he can guide others farther than he has gone himself. There may be other and more exoteric purposes for which the Grace is channelled through him, but as a guru he can only guide as far as he has gone. (And that was why Martin Lings warned me off my first *murshid*). That was the real ground for the Buddha's dissatisfaction with the gurus he went to before attaining Enlightenment. Finally (as may happen with the opener of a new path — as happened also with the Maharshi) he attained Enlightenment with no outer guru. The disciple who sets no limits to his aspiration needs a guru to whose achievement there are none.

Actually, recognition of a guru is complicated by impurities in the disciple which make him imagine perfection where it does not exist and overlook it where it does. There were many who did not recognize the Maharshi as a Guru and there are many who ascribe a high or the highest state to gurus who have only a formal legitimacy, if that.

The twofold possibility of finding a realized Guru and observing the orthodoxy of whatever religion he professed must have seemed pretty remote to many of Guenon's readers at the time when he wrote; it is vastly more so today, in view of the

100   *My Life and Quest*

rapid breakdown of tradition, drying up of spiritual streams and acceptance of modernism not only in the West but throughout the world and in all religions. To prevent despondency, Guenon gave the assurance that Christ's saying that whoever seeks shall find is a divine law of universal application. This implies, however, that there must be some technique by which it can still apply even in this present age, when a genuine guru has become so rare to find and orthodoxy, for most people, impracticable. Guenon never suggested what this technique might be or even seemed aware of the need for one. The adaptation necessary to meet the conditions of the new age was, of course, formless guidance, to which I referred briefly in 'Adventures on the Path', such as could reach the heart of whoever seeks, independent alike of religious orthodoxy and formal initiation. There may be various such currents of guidance in the world today; certainly one was instituted by the Maharshi.

In accordance with the needs of this path, he restored the term 'Guru' to its true and highest meaning, which is essentially the same as the Christian doctrine of 'the Christ in you'. This introduced a certain mystery into his use of the term. The following dialogue illustrates how it made the laying on of hands or transmission of a *mantram* by a human agent unnecessary:

Devotee: "Bhagavan has said that without the grace of the Guru one cannot attain to the Self. What precisely does he mean by this? What is this Guru?"

Bhagavan: "From the standpoint of the path of Knowledge, it is the supreme state of the Self. It is different from the ego, which you call your self."

Devotee: "Then if it is the supreme state of my own Self, in what sense does Bhagavan mean that I cannot reach it without the grace of the Guru?"

Arthur Osborne 101

Bhagavan: "The ego is the individuality and is not the same as the Lord of all. When it approaches the Lord with sincere devotion, he graciously assumes name and form and takes it to Himself. Therefore they say that the Guru is none other than the Lord. He is a human incarnation of Divine Grace."

A human incarnation, yes; but he also said that the Guru need not necessarily take human form; and since he shed the body the meaning of this saying has become clear.

It is obvious that this supreme definition of the Guru can apply only in a very limited way to one whose legitimacy depends on human appointment; in its fullness it can apply only to Bhagavan, to the *Jivan-Mukta* (emancipated while yet in the physical body). Bhagavan is indeed the universal divine Guru.

In another sense also he is universal. One who has attained the supreme state is above all the forms of religion. They are the paths leading up to the peak, but he is the peak itself, and everything else. A guru normally guides his followers along the path which he himself trod, and Bhagavan's approach to Realization was through an act of self-enquiry unconnected with the forms of the Hindu or any other religion. This also was what he taught. He came as an answer to the needs of our age, proclaiming a path which, with his grace and support can be followed by aspirants in any religion, and indeed whether they observed any formal religion or not.

It might be thought to follow from this that Bhagavan's initiation would be freely and openly given; on the contrary, it was concealed. Had it been open, the constant stream of visitors from India and abroad would have demanded it, putting Bhagavan under the necessity of accepting one and rejecting another; for ordinarily many seek initiation without pledging

102   *My Life and Quest*

themselves to the quest, merely as a sort of spiritual tonic. As it was, the aspirants' own understanding or lack of it performed the selection which in a secret order would be performed by the guru. Preparedness for initiation was the first hurdle, those who were not prepared never knowing that they had missed anything, and therefore not being subjected to jealousy, resentment or despondency, as they might otherwise have been.

If asked, Bhagavan would never deny that he gave initiation, but he would also not openly affirm it. The only time I have heard him do so was with Hartz. Sometimes he would answer that the Guru-disciple relationship is a reality from the point of view of the disciple and is necessary to him, although the Guru cannot affirm it, since for him there are no others and therefore there can be no relationship. It will be noted that Hartz's question was phrased in a form which made it possible to give an affirmative answer without any statement of relationship. This, of course, applies only to the perfect Guru who abides at all times in the state of Supreme Identity.

Nor was the initiation and guidance for Bhagavan's lifetime only. If it had been, it would have brought only a very temporary solution to the problem of modern world conditions. When asked: "Does the contact continue even after the dissolution of the physical body of the Guru or only so long as he is in the flesh and blood?" he answered: "The Guru is not the physical form; so contact will remain even after his physical form vanishes."

When his body's death seemed imminent and some devotees asked how they could pursue their *sadhana* without his continued guidance, he replied with the cryptic rebuke: "You attach too much importance to the body."

Indeed, one who has understood what is meant by the *Jivan-Mukta*, in constant, unwavering, conscious identity with

Arthur Osborne 103

the Self, does not need assurance; he understands that the presence or absence of a body can make no difference. "There are no stages in Self-realization. There are no degrees of liberation. So there cannot be one stage of liberation with the body and another when the body has been shed. The realized man knows that he is the Self and that nothing, neither his body nor anything else, exists but for the Self. To such a one what difference could the presence or absence of a body make?"

And in practise his devotees have found it so. Not only that, but new devotees continue to be drawn to him and experience his guidance as before. Many of those who come to Tiruvannamalai never saw him in his lifetime; many also follow his guidance from a distance, being unable to come. There are not the crowds that there were before, but many of these were sightseers who craved some limited blessing; the proportion of true devotees is higher now. The support and guidance is no less.

Being the universal Guru, Bhagavan proclaimed his teaching openly. It has been usual for a guru to maintain secrecy about methods of training, even though he might write openly on theory; indeed this precaution was necessary, since it was illegitimate and might be dangerous to practise any technique without personal authorisation. Under Bhagavan's guidance, however, understanding and aspiration are the only qualifications and their absence the only barriers.

A visitor once asked him: "May I be assured that there is nothing further to be learnt, so far as the technique of spiritual practise is concerned, than what was written in Bhagavan's books?" He further explained, "I ask because in all other systems the guru holds back some secret technique to reveal to his disciples at the time of initiation."

104   *My Life and Quest*

And Bhagavan replied: "There is nothing more to be known than what you find in the books. No secret technique. It is all an open secret in this system."

Open and yet secret, because, although expressed openly, few seem to understand all the implications.

The method is Self-enquiry: Who am I?

Sometimes he would say: "Whether or not you believe in the reality of the world or of God, you know that you exist, so start with yourself and find out first who you are."

Who am I? What is the reality of me? Not my body, because it changes constantly from youth to age, from sickness to health, but I still am. Besides, I say that I have a body, not that I am one, and what I have is not what I am. Who is it that says 'my head', 'my hands', 'my body'? Also not my thoughts and feelings, ambitions and desires, likes and dislikes, hopes and fears: all these stay with me for a while and then pass away; those I have now are quite different from what I had ten years ago; but I still am. Besides, I have none of them when in a deep, dreamless sleep, and yet I still exist. And of them also I say 'I have', not 'I am'. What, then, am I? What remains when all that is adventitious has been taken away?

All this is not what Bhagavan meant by Self-enquiry. It is a useful mental introduction to it, but Self-enquiry, as he taught it, is not a mental but a spiritual exercise. Therefore any mental or verbal answer must be wrong. 'Any answer the mind can give is wrong.' To give an answer means mistaking for a philosophical conundrum what is in fact a spiritual exercise.

"The enquiry 'Who am I?' really means trying to find the source of the ego or 'I'-thought. You are not to occupy the mind with other thoughts such as 'I am not the body'. Seeking the source of the 'I' serves as a means of getting rid of all other thoughts."

Arthur Osborne 105

It is also not a psychological study or a technique for getting to know one's qualities or aptitudes or uncovering one's subconscious urges, but for realizing the Self behind the ego that has these qualities and urges. "Just as it is futile to examine the rubbish that has to be swept up only to be thrown away, so it is futile for him who seeks to know the Self to set to work enumerating the *tattvas* that envelop the Self and examining them instead of throwing them away."

Nor is it one 'I' seeking for another. There is only one Self in you, not two.

A visitor once asked: "Isn't it funny that I should be searching for the 'I'? Doesn't the enquiry 'Who am I?' turn out in the end to be an empty formula? Or am I to put the question to myself endlessly, repeating it like an incantation?"

And he was told: "Self-enquiry is certainly not an empty formula; it is more than the repetition of an incantation. If it were mere mental questioning it would not be of much value. Its very purpose is to focus the entire mind at its source. It is not therefore a case of one 'I' searching for another. Still less is it an empty formula, for it involves intense activity of the entire mind to keep it steadily poised in pure Self-awareness. Self-enquiry is the one infallible means, the only direct one, to realize the unconditioned, absolute Being that you really are."

Just as aspirants were warned not to make a mental investigation out of Self-enquiry, so also they are warned not to make an incantation out of it and not to confuse it with the meditation 'I am He'. "Self-enquiry is a different method from the meditation 'I am Shiva' or 'I am He'. It rather lays stress on Self-knowledge, because you are first concerned with yourself before you proceed to know the world and its Lord. The 'I am He' or 'I am Brahman' meditation is more or less

106 *My Life and Quest*

mental, but the quest of the Self is a direct method and is superior to it."

Usually a man's mind is turned outwards, creating or following a course of action or of thought. Instead of that it is to be turned inwards upon itself, asking 'Who am I?', not seeking an answer to the question but simply experiencing the sense of awareness, of I-am-ness, letting that alone remain in the consciousness.

Man has three functions: action, thought and being. Being underlies the other two and is the necessary substratum for them, and yet is almost completely overshadowed by them, so that it is very rarely that a man is aware of actual being, of his pure I-am-ness. To use a simile that Bhagavan often made use of: it is like a cinema screen on which a film is shown. The spectators are not aware of it but only of the pictures passing across it; and yet it is real and they are shadows on it; it exists unchanged before the showing of the film and while the pictures are moving across it and after they have come to an end. And it is quite unaffected by them: a fire in the picture does not burn it nor a flood make it wet.

It is this awareness of being that is to be cultivated. It is developed by Self-enquiry; indeed, the quest for it is itself a mode of Self-enquiry. Sometimes Bhagavan would say: "Your duty is simply to be; not to be this or that." And therefore he would quote as the perfect name of God 'I am that I am'. He also often quoted the sentence from the Psalms: 'Be still and know that I am God'. Keep the mind still, free from thoughts, and know that the 'I am', the pure Being, is God.

Bhagavan used the term 'meditation' for the practise of Self-enquiry, and that term is used in this book also, but it does not mean meditation as a dictionary would define it. It is not

Arthur Osborne 107

meditating on anything or concentrating on any one thought. It is different in kind from the Sufi meditation I described in an earlier chapter, since it is not thinking but suspending or stilling thoughts while holding the mind alert in quest of itself, or in pure awareness of being, of I-am-ness.

So far is Self-enquiry from being a mental exercise that Bhagavan enjoined those who used it to concentrate not on the head but the heart during meditation. This does not mean thinking of the heart or trying to visualize or imagine it, for that would be a mental exercise. You do not think of the eyes or visualize them in order to see; you simply look with them. And in the same way the sense of awareness starts simply by concentrating on the heart which is all pervading. Simply to sit concentrating one's sense of 'I'-ness, of being, in the heart and at the same time asking, 'Who am I?' — not constantly but just once, in order to hold the mind in that direction, repeating the thought only as a weapon to drive out other thoughts when they arise.

Moreover, when Bhagavan spoke of concentration on the heart he did not mean the physical heart on the left side but the centre of spiritual awareness at the right side of the chest. Some of the ashram publications refer in this connection to the verse from Ecclesiastes: 'The wise man's heart is at the right hand and the fool's heart is at the left.' (Ch.X, v.2, authorized version). This centre is not one of the yogic *chakras*. The direct method is not concerned with them or with the *kundalini* technique. The following dialogue explains this:

Devotee: "Bhagavan was saying that the heart is the seat or centre of the Self?"

Bhagavan: "Yes, it is the one supreme centre of the Self. You need have no doubts about that. The real Self is there in the heart behind the ego-self."

108   *My Life and Quest*

Devotee: "Will Bhagavan please tell me where in the body it is?"

Bhagavan: "You cannot know with your mind or picture it with your imagination, although I tell you that it is here (pointing to the right side of the chest). The only direct way to realize it is to stop imagining and try to be yourself. Then you automatically feel that the centre is there. It is the centre spoken of in the scriptures as the heart-cavity."

Devotee: "Can I be sure that the ancients meant this centre by the term 'heart'?"

Bhagavan: "Yes, you can; but you should try to have the experience rather than locate it. A man does not have to go and find where his eyes are in order to see. The heart is there, always open to you, if you care to enter it, always supporting your movements, although you may be unaware of it. It is perhaps more correct to say that the Self is the heart. Really the Self is the centre and is everywhere aware of itself as the Heart or Self-awareness."

Devotee: "When Bhagavan says that the heart is the supreme centre of the Spirit or Self, does that imply that it is not one of the six *chakras* (yogic centres)?"

Bhagavan: "The *chakras*, counting from the bottom upwards, are a series of centres in the (subtle) nervous system. They represent various stages, each having its own kind of power or knowledge, leading to the *sahasrara*, the thousand-petalled lotus in the brain, where is seated the supreme *Shakti* (Divine Energy). But the Self that supports the whole movement of the *Shakti* is not located there but supports it from the heart-centre."

Devotee: "Then it is different from the manifestation of *Shakti*?"

Bhagavan: "Really there is no manifestation of *Shakti* apart from the Self. It is the Self that becomes all these *shaktis*. When

Arthur Osborne 109

the yogi attains the highest state of spiritual awareness (*samadhi*) it is the Self in the heart that supports him in that state, whether he is aware of it or not. But if his awareness is centred in the heart he realizes that, whatever centres or states he may be in, he is always the same Truth, the same Heart, the one Self, the Spirit that is present throughout, eternal and immutable."

More specifically, he explained on another occasion: "The *sushumna* is thus a curve. It starts from the solar plexus, rises through the spinal cord to the brain, and from there bends down and ends in the heart. When the yogi has reached the heart the *samadhi* becomes permanent. Thus we see that the heart is the final centre." (It is interesting to note that Lama Govinda explains similarly in his *Foundations of Tibetan Mysticism* that on the Tibetan path epitomised by the incantation 'Om Mani Padme Hum' the initiate, after attaining the highest centre, which is in the brain, comes down to the heart for final stabilisation. Unfortunately he presents this knowledge as exclusive to Tantric Buddhism. Obviously, no truth of general application can be confined to any one religion or path).

The above dialogue indicates a technical explanation why there are no stages on the direct path. There is no successive development of the various subtle centres, each of which has its own types of power and perception; instead there is concentration from the beginning on the Self to which all powers belong and the Heart from which all centres radiate and by which they are supported.

Self-enquiry is, of course, not a new method. Being the most direct method, it must be the oldest. In ancient times, however, it was a path for the recluse striving in silence and solitude; but in more recent ages diminishing spirituality has

110   *My Life and Quest*

caused it to be little used. What Bhagavan did was to restore it as a method that can be used in the conditions of the modern world. Its independence of doctrine and ritual, in fact its primordiality, already made it potentially universal; and Bhagavan further adapted it by combining it with *karma-marga*, that is with progress through activity. Not only did he not expect his followers to renounce the world, but also when they asked his sanction to do so, he refused.

"Why do you think you are a householder? The similar thought that you are a hermit will haunt you if you go forth as one. Whether you continue in the household or renounce it and go to live in the forest, your mind haunts you. The ego is the source of thought. It creates the body and the world and makes you think you are a householder. If you renounce, it will only substitute the thought of renunciation for that of family, and the environment of the forest for that of the household. The mental obstacles are always there for you. They even increase greatly in the new surroundings. Change of environment is no help. The one obstacle is the mind, and this must be overcome whether in the home or in the forest. If you can do it in the forest, why not in the home? So why change the environment? Your efforts can be made even now, whatever the environment."

And when asked whether it is possible to experience *samadhi* or spiritual awareness while working he replied: "It is the feeling 'I work' that is the hindrance. Ask yourself 'Who works?' Remember who you are. Then the work will not bind you; it will go on automatically."

Similarly, he did not insist on celibacy. Indeed, in traditional Hindu society all householders are married; only the *sadhu,* the world-renouncer, is a celibate; and it was this

Arthur Osborne 111

outer renunciation which he discouraged. Inner detachment is the real renunciation.

Sometimes he gave the example of the actor on the stage, playing a certain part as the author has written it, although knowing that he is not really that person; sometimes of a bank cashier who pays out thousands coolly and efficiently, knowing that it is not his money that he is paying.

The usual way is to devote a certain time to meditation daily, for instance in the early morning and the evening, and for the rest of the time to try and remember during the activities of the day. At first this remembering is mainly a mental and moral discipline — 'who is flattered by this attention, pleased by this letter, slighted by so-and-so's action? Who am I?' After some practise, however, it takes a deeper tone, becoming an extension of the more potent meditation.

Few of Bhagavan's devotees lived permanently at Tiruvannamalai. It was (and still is) more usual to live in the world, engaged in some business or profession, and pay only occasional visits, to re-charge the batteries, so to speak.

Although Bhagavan spoke and wrote mostly of Self-enquiry, that is, of the 'Path of Knowledge', he recognised also the path of love and devotion among his followers. To some who took this path he has made the tremendous statement: "Submit to me and I will strike down the mind," or: "Only keep quiet and I will do the rest." But it is not easy to submit or to keep the mind quiet.

These different paths are not mutually exclusive in practise, although they might theoretically appear to be.

To return to my story.

Throughout the years of our separation my wife never doubted Bhagavan's guidance. She had complete faith in him.

112   *My Life and Quest*

When I joined her after the war and suggested showing him a photo of Martin's guru and telling him that this was our guru, she was horrified. "But you can't possibly do that!" she exclaimed. "How could you tell Bhagavan that somebody else is our guru?"

"But he himself is not a guru," I protested with crude logic, repeating what I had been told.

"But you can't possibly do that!" she repeated. "It would be a terrible thing to do."

And I didn't.

Nevertheless, despite her complete reliance on Bhagavan, she continued the exercises into which we had been initiated and never found it necessary to write to Martin about the change of allegiance. For someone as indifferent as she was to the theory of initiation and guru, and who, moreover, until coming to Bhagavan, and been so half-hearted about the whole matter, such behaviour was quite natural; but could I do the same?

I soon found that I could not continue the practises into which I had been initiated and which represented a different and less direct path. They became a terrible drag and burden on me. I forced myself to continue them for some time out of a sense of duty and then asked Bhagavan's permission to drop them. He gave it, saying: "Yes, all other methods lead up to Self-enquiry."

There was never any question of becoming a Hindu, which (even supposing it were possible) would have meant taking on myself a new burden of formalities.

I felt therefore an obligation to inform the guru through whom, even though indirectly, the exercises had been prescribed, since it was in effect a change of allegiance. There was also the question of correcting Guenon's mistake. Not only did I owe that to him, since it was he who had brought me forth from a life of

Arthur Osborne 113

ignorance to quest for the Goal, and thereby indirectly to Bhagavan, but there was the consideration of all the others who were inspired by him to seek a path and yet, by this mistake of his, might find the path blocked by his 'no road' sign, as I had so nearly done.

It must be remembered that Guenon was strongly opposed to modern empirical methods of thinking, instead of which he advocated the traditional method of understanding the basic principles and applying them to actual circumstances. He usually did this successfully, but I have already mentioned instances in which this was not the case, by applying principles in too doctrinaire a manner. It now transpired that his mistaken denial of Bhagavan as a Guru had more serious implications because it was likely to have graver practical repercussions on those seeking guidance. Initiation had always been transmitted through strictly orthodox channels and in a formal manner; Bhagavan's initiation and guidance was not formal and did not follow the orthodoxy of any religion; therefore, he argued, it did not exist. It did not occur to him that since most of the orthodox channels had dried up, and the waters of life which they formerly conveyed had become inaccessible to almost all mankind, the Divine Grace might have opened a new path in accordance with the needs of the age. He often referred to such a phenomenon, to the outpouring of Grace being channelled in a new way to suit the conditions of a different age or community, but he did not admit or perceive that this had happened in his own age also. Of course, what he ought to have done before issuing such a grave denial was to come and verify for himself, but, as with his rejection of Buddhism, this was just what he would not do, as it smacked of empiricism.

I decided that I should write a letter to Martin to be shown to his guru and Guenon, explaining that Bhagavan was a Guru and did give initiation and guidance.

However, there was one great impediment to this. As I have already stated, one of Guenon's enthusiasts had been to Tiruvannamalai and, failing to understand the silent initiation and guidance, had reported back that there was none and that Bhagavan was not a Guru.

Could I expect Guenon to take my word against his, especially when his confirmed Guenon's theory and mine refuted it? It seemed most unlikely. I therefore wrote a letter containing the definite statement that Bhagavan was a Guru and did give initiation and guidance and showed it to Bhagavan, asking his permission to send it. Although he did not normally give any affirmation in this matter, I hoped that, in view of the importance of the case, he would make an exception, He did. He read the letter through carefully, handed it back and said: "Yes, send it." I sent the letter to Martin with a postscript explaining this.

Bhagavan himself never wrote letters; therefore a letter sent with his express authorisation could be taken as a message from him. The last chapter of Guenon's *Man and His Becoming According to Vedanta* showed that he understood what was meant by the *Jivan-Mukta*, the Divine Man fully Self-realized. Now he would be receiving a personal message from one. I hoped that he would accept it and not make himself like those who had denied Christ because he did not come in the form they had expected.

11

I Become a Writer—and Cease to Be One

IN MY YOUTH I was tormented by the desire to be a writer. When I actually became one, some twenty years later, it happened almost by accident — so far as anything can be an accident; that is to say, without planning on my part.

After two to three years at Tiruvannamalai it became necessary to earn an income again and I took a job as an assistant editor of a newspaper in Madras, the nearest large town. Thus my destiny took the shape that Bhagavan approved for his followers — a period of intensive training followed by the practise of Self-enquiry in the life of the world.

I took with me a life-sized reproduction of the photograph painted over in oils, a gift from a devotee who had, over the years amassed a fine collection of pictures of Bhagavan. Before leaving I showed it to Bhagavan who took it in his hands and then gave it back to me, saying: "He is taking Swami with him."

116   *My Life and Quest*

Such was the impersonal way in which he would speak of himself. After that it had a peculiar significance for me. It is one of the most inward and profound of the portraits, though less obviously gracious and immediately accessible than some of the others.

I took to journalism immediately. I should never have had the effrontery to make a good reporter, but fortunately that was not necessary; and editorial work came naturally to me as teaching never had. I doubt whether, before this, I should have been capable of writing either a book or an article successfully; my style was too subjective and abstract; but under the impulse of professional need I straight away began to write professionally. The editing of contributed articles, deciding which were written in a practical way and what changes were needed, taught me also to write in a practical way, and almost without effort. Perhaps this was a training in the technique of writing to enable me to write later about Bhagavan and his teaching.

I scanned the papers and wrote leaders, but in particular I took over and developed the Sunday magazine section, including a book review page. It was in this way, not as a student but as a critic, that I broke my long abstention from reading. Even after giving up journalism as a profession I continued to review books for various papers and therefore still read widely, but in a haphazard way, never buying books or borrowing them from libraries, only reading what came my way for review. Primarily these were books of spiritual interest, and indeed for a number of years most new publications of this type came to me, but I received many other books also — history, politics, current affairs, various branches of philosophy, even books of travel and fiction — and thus I became well read again. I read aloofly, scanning as a critic, not letting myself get engrossed, so that there could be no distraction from the quest, and therefore the

Arthur Osborne 117

type of writing for which I was suited was critical and analytical, not creative. It would have saved a lot of heartache if I had known myself well enough to realize this earlier in life. How many people bring frustration on themselves by trying to be what they are not, instead of developing what they are! "Better one's own dharma, though done badly, than the dharma of another, though done well." (*Bhagavad Gita*, Ch. 12, v. 47). It is seldom done well.

It was only now, in my Madras period, that I became a complete vegetarian. Physical disciplines are, of course, much less important on the direct path of Self-enquiry than on any other, but one which Bhagavan did lay stress on was vegetarianism. The most obvious motive for it is compassion — not merely personal compassion for the beasts slaughtered; that also, of course, but beneath it is the more intellectual compassion of equal-mindedness, seeing the same sanctity in all life and not consenting that other creatures should be deprived of theirs in order to sustain mine own. Even apart from that, however, vegetarianism is in one's mind as well as body. Animal food is deleterious for spiritual development; it sets up an undesirable vibration or magnetism and the mind imbibes the wrong qualities. Whenever any one asked Bhagavan about it, he always and quite definitely recommended vegetarianism. It is also characteristic of his wisdom and patience that if any one did not ask, he did not enjoin it. It is the tree that produces the fruit, not the fruit the tree. To impose vegetarianism from above might lead to suppressed resentment which would smoulder and increase; it was better to wait till the inner development demanded it.

I had been a great meat-eater all my life, taking meat daily, often, in one form or another, three times a day, morning, noon and night, except for a short period at Oxford when I had been a vegetarian as a result of reading Leonardo da Vinci's saying that we are all cemeteries of dead animals. At Tiruvannamalai we ate less meat than ever before but did not completely renounce it. By the time we moved to Madras we had given up cooking meat at home, but every Tuesday I used to go into town at lunchtime to lay my weekly stock of tobacco, and I would eat a meat lunch at a restaurant. One Tuesday I ordered a chicken *pilau* but when it arrived I felt that I just could not face the thought of eating it. It was not any theoretical objection or even any feeling of compassion for this chicken, just an inner revulsion. So I sent it back and ordered fried fish instead. Next Tuesday I repeated this order, but I had the same feeling about that also and sent it back. I never ate meat or fish again. The meditation sets up a finer vibration and in some ways makes one more sensitive to food and environment. The point had been reached when vegetarianism had become a necessity.

Another effect of the quest is that the repercussion of one's actions, favourable or unfavourable, recompense or retribution, becomes more swift and recognizable. Every action brings its repercussions ("As a man sows so shall he reap"), that is the law of karma, but in the spiritually ignorant and the worldly it may be so long delayed and heavily masked as not to be recognized by the person himself. As one becomes more deliberately equipoised, much less impurity is sufficient to cause disequilibrium, just as a delicate machine can be thrown out of gear by an impediment too minute to affect a heavier, clumsier machine. Also the repercussions follow more swiftly in a more recognized form.

My Tuesday lunches in town soon ceased to be necessary in any case, because I gave up smoking. Ever since Oxford I had

Arthur Osborne 119

been a heavy pipe-smoker. Even in the internment camp in Thailand, I was able to get pipe tobacco most of the time, and when it was not available I smoked Burmese cheroots or fat Thai cigarettes wrapped in banana-leaf.

After some practise the meditation sets up a sort of current of awareness which can actually be felt physically as a vibration. At first it is felt only during meditation and only in the heart and head and between them, but gradually it becomes more pervasive and more constant, forming a sort of undercurrent to one's life and actions. Smoking also is a sort of undercurrent, so I felt that it was a spurious imitation, an actual impurity, once the meditational vibration was awakened. I had twice before in my life given up smoking. Both times I started again about six months later. This time, however, it was final. I did not even wait to finish the tobacco in my pouch. I gave it away with the remaining tobacco in it and all my pipes to a young journalist, who fancied himself as a pipe-smoker — perhaps because it made him look English — and never smoked again, or even wanted to.

This current of awareness of which I speak could not be called exactly a pleasure, and yet one would not barter it for any pleasure imaginable. Thus faded out the question that had confronted me when I first undertook the quest: whether I was prepared to sacrifice pleasures I knew to be real for pleasures that might be real.

My wife was not with me at all constantly in Madras. The children were still at school in the hills and expected her to spend the hot months there with them, and she also wanted to stay some time at Tiruvannamalai. We had had difficulty with accommodation and so now, while I was at Madras, she built a house there. She had firm faith that we should eventually be able to retire and settle down there, unlikely as it seemed at

120 *My Life and Quest*

the time. She engaged no architect and drew up no blueprints, just told the masons what to do next, and yet it turned out a delightful little house, beautiful and compact, a palace the size of a doll's house.

I have told elsewhere the story of Bhagavan's long and painful illness and his leaving the body (see my *Ramana Maharshi and the Path of Self-Knowledge*) and will not repeat it here. In 1949 and 1950 my wife, like other devotees, was reluctant to leave Tiruvannamalai longer than necessary. I used to go for occasional weekends and holidays. I was there on the occasion of one of the operations. Immediately after it, Bhagavan's couch was carried out on to the veranda of the dispensary where the operation took place. He looked exhausted. I ascended the few steps. He had not known that I was in Tiruvannamalai and as I came before him his face lit up with a smile of radiant beauty. I stood there, looking at him, overwhelmed by what transpired, by the undeserved grace.

We were there when he left the body, in April 1950. After that every one seemed anxious to get away. The place became deserted. I was able to stay for a few days and then my leave expired. My wife stayed on. Neither of us felt any gloom, any vacuum. The whole place was radiant with his presence. Never had the vibration of peace been so pervasive or so powerful. He had said: "They say that I am going away, but where can I go? I am here." The 'here' is universal, the infinite here and now of the Spirit; but it also meant Tiruvannamalai, as it had in his body's lifetime. Gradually others also began to feel it and to come back and the place filled up again. New devotees also began to be drawn there, both from India and abroad, and the movement has continued.

Arunachala Hill, with the town of Tiruvannamalai at its foot, is one of the most ancient spiritual centres in India. It is

Arthur Osborne 121

peculiarly associated with the direct path of Self-enquiry and the silent initiation connected with this. Indeed, it is the traditional centre of Dakshinamurti, who is Siva teaching in silence in the form of a youthful Guru with aged disciples. That is why Bhagavan was drawn there and made it his home and why he wrote hymns to Arunachala as a form assumed by Siva, the Formless God. Perhaps it is also why Arunachala has been less well known than other centres such as Benares and Mt. Kailash — the direct path of self-enquiry has been less accessible and less widespread than other, indirect paths. Now, however, since Bhagavan has restored it and simplified it to suit the spirit of our age, Arunachala has once again become the active spiritual centre. Bhagavan has said that it is the centre of the world. People who come here feel a potency and beauty and a tremendous vibration of peace.

After his death I wrote a number of articles about Bhagavan for my own paper and others. The ashram wanted to continue publishing as a sign that it was still flourishing, and I collected these together and edited them to form the chapters of a book which I called *Ramana Arunachala* and gave to the ashram to publish, taking no royalties for it. So, almost by accident, my first book was published.

There already was an official ashram life of Bhagavan, but it only went up to 1936 and was written in a florid Indian imitation of Victorian verbosity. I was asked whether I could revise it and bring it up to date. At first I agreed, but when I got down to work I found that so much needed to be changed, both in style and structure, that the only thing to do was to write a new book. So my second book came to be written, *Ramana Maharshi and the Path of Self-Knowledge*, the first half of it largely, though not exclusively, based on the previous ashram biography.

Before it was ready for publication some one told Gerald Yorke of Rider & Co. about it and so he wrote to me suggesting that I should get it published in England, so that it could be given proper publicity and serve to make Bhagavan and his teaching known outside India also. I immediately agreed and gave the royalties of this book also to the ashram.

Rider's were at the time publishing rather second rate occultist stuff, and I was not pleased to have a life of Bhagavan brought out by them; but Yorke was reading manuscripts for them and trying to raise their standard. A year or two later he became publications manager for the firm and, with the help of others on the staff, succeeded in his efforts so considerably that they became one of the most outstanding publishers of books of real spiritual interest and a pleasant firm to deal with in every way. My correspondence with Yorke continues and I always found him friendly and helpful. Several times I was able to refer people to him when they wrote to me from England about the possibilities of spiritual affiliation.

It was in 1950, before this book came out, that we sent Catherine and Adam, the two eldest children, to England to finish their education.

Had conditions been different, this might have been my last job. As it was, it became necessary to leave in 1952. I had an offer of a post on better conditions as principal of a high school in Calcutta. With Adam to pay for in England that was quite a consideration. Catherine had been staying with my parents and she finished school and returned to us before the end of 1952, but Adam had longer to go and then had to go on to university.

After I had left the paper, the management of the school I was to take over vacillated and postponed, so it was already 1953

Arthur Osborne 123

before we went to Calcutta. Thus the last job I was to take up followed the pattern of my whole professional career — that each successive post was not only a new job but also a new kind of job, and that each job lasted four years.

I found the work interesting. The work of the head of a school is quite different from that of a teacher, in fact mainly organization and administration. And this job also I found of value in my own development, in developing the qualities of decisiveness and organizational ability which had remained latent. Does it sound odd to speak of work helping the development of one's character in one's late forties? Anyway, so it was. There are two explanations, one personal and the other general: the former is that altogether I matured late, the latter that a person who has undertaken the quest does not ossify with advancing years but remains in a constant state of development. The school was drying up from the base when I took over, the two lowest classes both being below strength; when I left it five years later it had more than doubled in numbers.

Catherine also took a job in Calcutta. At the beginning of 1955 she married and left for Peshawar with her husband who had a job there.

Ever since I came to India I had been hearing of a bizarre saint known as Sai Baba, who not only never wrote a book but never read one. He lived in a mosque but was worshipped there by Hindus, making his Hindu and Muslim disciples live peaceably side by side. He performed a reckless profusion of miracles but justified them with the profound saying: "I give people what they want so that they will begin to want what I want to give them." He would fly into a rage and abuse or even beat his devotees, and yet he was all love. He would ask for money (a thing a saint in India never does) and yet it was all

124   *My Life and Quest*

distributed among the poor, and he himself would go out and beg his food. He died as long ago as 1918 in the little town of Shirdi near Bombay, where he had spent his life, and yet as far south as Madras I found his bust or portrait in house after house, shop after shop, with incense sticks burning in front of it.

Moreover, in four important respects he seemed a precursor of Bhagavan in adapting spiritual training to the conditions of the modern world. Like Bhagavan, he gave no formal initiation; like Bhagavan, he had disciples of different religions; like Bhagavan, he did not encourage them to renounce the world. And finally, he also continued to guide his disciples and to attract new ones after physical death. In hearing or reading the many stories of his appearance to devotees in dream or vision or in physical form and of his miraculous intervention in sickness or misfortune, there is no barrier at 1918; the same sort of cases occur after this date as before, and are just as frequent.

He probably has a larger following in India than any other saint, but is almost unknown in the West, perhaps because he has no philosophy or written teaching to comment on. There was no readable book about him in English and I had long felt the need for one. I even wrote an article to that effect to an Indian periodical. I sent a copy of it to Yorke, hoping that he might be able to find somebody to undertake the task. I felt that the life of so vivid and bizarre a saint should be written by some one with a more colourful style than mine. However, I saw eventually that if it was going to be done I should have to do it myself. So I wrote my next book, *The Incredible Sai Baba*. It was published in Calcutta by Orient Longmans, the eastern offshoot of Longman Green. By arrangement with them, Riders also published an edition for sale in England. By this time I was headmaster of the school in Calcutta.

Arthur Osborne 125

Now that the beloved face was no longer with us, my wife at last started work on the long delayed sculpture. It was felt that there should be a statue of Bhagavan and the ashram had several times commissioned one, but the results were deplorable. One can measure features, but to reproduce the expression of the Divine Man would require love and understanding. My wife got some clay and started work on a bust. For over a year she worked at it, never quite satisfied, always changing and perfecting. Finally the face came to have a beautiful expression reminiscent of the living Bhagavan, but the poise of the head and shoulders was still not right. Then she went to Tiruvannamalai for a few weeks and it dried up and cracked. The face fell off in one unbroken piece, while the rest broke into bits. Taking this as a sign, we made a plaster cast of the face alone.

I had no intention of becoming a writing addict and going on with book after book. However, there were two more books that I wanted to get written. Both of them were ideas that had been in my mind ever since I was in the internment camp; which means that both were legacies from the period of Guenon's influence and were concerned rather with contingent matters than with the path and its technique. I had vaguely hoped through the years that I should meet some scholar to whom I could pass them on, but had not considered writing them myself. I saw now, however, that they would not be written unless I did it, and, having a connection now with two publishers, I decided to do so. I was so familiar with them that it was rather a case of writing out than writing; nevertheless an idea is vitally affected by the crystallisation of form-giving and there was quite a lot of work to do — work which I found enthralling.

The first to be written was called *The Rhythm of History* and was published by Orient Longmans in Calcutta. I was not

126   *My Life and Quest*

joining the ranks of historians who try to decide what this rhythm is, but simply indicating that if the history of the various civilizations of mankind falls into any uniform pattern at all, and if this pattern cannot be ascribed to mutual influences or to progress, there must be some meaning or harmony underlying it; it cannot be a mere succession of blind accidents. That there is such a pattern is clear but has been rather overlooked by historians. I began with the amazing coincidence of the founding or re-founding of religions and civilizations about the 5th century before Christ — Lao Tsu and Confucius in China, Buddha and Mahavir in India, probably Zoroaster in Persia, Ezekial and the Deutero-Isaiah and return from the Babylonian Captivity among the Jews, Pythagoras in Greece, the founding of the Roman Republic, at all approximately the same time. Then, midway between this time and the time of Christ, there was the creation of great empires which served the diffusion and interconnection of the new cultural patterns, although not created for that purpose — Alexander's Empire stretching from Greece to India, that of Asoka in India, the unification of China by the Chin, followed by the Han Dynasty with its state patronage of Taoism and Confucianism. The next wave is the contemporaneous infiltration of the young Roman Empire and the West by Christianity and of the young Han Empire and the East by Mahayana Buddhism. Then all the classical civilizations alike fell into dark times, times of turbulence and governmental impotence. Out of this eventually rose recognizably mediaeval types of civilization — in China, in India, in Islam, in Christendom, everywhere. The Renaissance also was a worldwide phenomenon, only in the West it triumphed whereas in all Eastern civilizations Counter-Reformatory movements suppressed it. This led to an end in the present century by the

Arthur Osborne 127

uniform acceptance of the modern, materialistic, mechanized, utilitarian type of civilization without spiritual foundations.

There was, of course, much more detail, but it was still a slim book. It might have been better if it had been twice the length or more, based on more erudition, but I have not the disposition of a research worker. It said more than I now consider wise about the world being ripe for the coming of the Tenth Avatar. Whether that is so or not, it may unsettle an already unsettled age to talk about it and thus do more harm than good.

The next book was *Buddhism and Christianity in the Light of Hinduism* and was published by Riders. Although refuting Guenon's condemnation of Buddhism (by implication but without actually referring to his statements) it was considerably influenced by his teaching, as was my whole outlook.

Outwardly there is an extraordinary parallel between Buddhism and Christianity. Each in its own way relaxes the rigour and simplifies the complexity of the law, instituting instead a new form of religion based on the love or compassion of the founder. Both, as originally propounded, were religions of renunciation, favouring celibacy and leading naturally to monasticism. Both proved unacceptable to the people among whom they were proclaimed but provided a sort of 'export variety' of the older religion for adoption by the neighbouring peoples who had lost the spiritual plenitude of their own religions.

In doctrine, on the other hand, they appear so mutually exclusive that one might be tempted to suppose that if one is true the other must be false, were it not for the sight of both types of doctrine existing side by side in Hinduism, both recognized as orthodox. Buddhism teaches non-duality and the dissolution of the individual being in Nirvana; Christianity, duality and the perpetuation of the purified individual being in a formal heaven. Actually, I had first envisaged the book simply as a comparison of Buddhism and Christianity; only later it occurred to me that reference to the co-existence of the two types of doctrine in Hinduism, non-dualism and dualism, knowledge and worship, both recognized as valid and sometimes even taught by the same guru, according to the needs and understanding of the disciples, would make it much easier to explain how both alike could be valid paths.

In this book some reference to the doctrine of avatars was a necessary part of the theme. The word is used rather loosely nowadays, but technically there are ten avatars in the whole course of the *manvantara*, that is, of the Adamic cycle. The seventh is Rama, whose story is told in the *Ramayana*. The eight is Krishna and its gospel the *Bhagavad Gita*. The function of the tenth, who is still to come, is the consummation of this cycle and inauguration of the next, which means that he is equivalent to the Second Coming of Christ. The ninth is described traditionally as the 'Foreign Avatar'. It is generally agreed he has already appeared, and he is sometimes identified with Buddha, sometimes with Christ. My thesis was that the ninth avatar consists of the twofold establishment of a proselytising religion based on the love or compassion of the founder, in the form of Buddhism and non-duality for the East, Christianity and the dualistic worship of a personal God for the West.

Having finished *Buddhism and Christianity*, I decided that I would not write another book unless the time came when I should be able to write one purely of guidance on the quest and should feel that it was legitimate for me to do so. As I have already explained, outer activity is useful on Bhagavan's path, but it should be aloof activity which keeps the mind working smoothly on the surface while underneath the current of meditation can continue. Emotionally involved activity, on the other hand, is harmful, since it turns the mind outwards, absorbing it in the activity and thereby impeding spiritual progress. Such activity may be of various kinds, but three of them are particularly dangerous, and also particularly alluring. Two of these I have mentioned already: reading and acting the guru; writing is the third.

It is not reading itself that is harmful but absorption in it — unless, of course, it is the sort of reading that serves as a spiritual reminder, turning the mind in the right direction. The sort of aloof, critical reading that I was doing remained a surface activity and could do no harm.

Similarly, there is no harm in giving help and advice on the path when the need to do so comes one's way; but one who makes himself responsible for the spiritual welfare of others is turning his mind outwards, entangling it in worry and anxiety, and thereby impeding his own progress.

Writing also is an activity into which a man normally throws himself whole-heartedly and which therefore impedes his spiritual progress. I felt that I should desist.

The same thing can be expressed in a more doctrinal way. It is not actions that impede one's *sadhana* or spiritual strife but the *vasanas*, that is the deep-seated desires or tendencies giving rise to the actions. Indeed, *sadhana* is sometimes represented simply as the elimination of *vasanas*, since it is these which turn the mind outwards, fling one into unnecessary activity, and drag the consciousness back to re-birth after this life has finished. Aloof or routine activity which does not nourish the *vasanas* is harmless; only emotional activity is dangerous. This also explains why unintelligent asceticism (not that all asceticism need be

130   *My Life and Quest*

unintelligent) fails of its purpose: it attacks the actions produced by the *vasanas* instead of the *vasanas* themselves, which may drive them to seek other outlets or to grow and fester in the dark. Intelligent self-discipline, whether asceticism or not, attacks the *vasanas* themselves. Self-enquiry, the most direct and efficacious method, does not even do that; it dispels the illusion of the ego which has the *vasanas*. Restricting activity is like trying to kill a tree by picking off the flowers and fruit; attacking the *vasanas* is like breaking off the branches; Self-enquiry is like uprooting the tree.

The worst method is to try to destroy the *vasanas* by gratifying them. That has the opposite effect, like trying to put a fire out by pouring oil on it. Nevertheless, it may happen that indulging it can finally exorcise a more or less innocuous remnant of a *vasana*. I think it is Sri Ramakrishna of whom the story is told that he had once desired a silk shawl and a gold chain, so he asked for them and sat on the bank of the Ganges wearing them; then, saying, "Now I have had my desire," he took them off and threw them into the Ganges. It is possible that in a similar way the writing of these books extinguished what vestige still remained of the urge to write. However, to have continued would have fanned the flame again.

At the same time that I stopped writing, and for the same reason, my wife gave up painting. She had not previously known that she could paint. Indeed, when she was young it was music that was her great passion and to which she would have dedicated her life had circumstances been propitious. However, in Calcutta, Frania, our youngest daughter, began to take art lessons and, in order to encourage her and find out her difficulties, my wife also began to paint and found that she could. When we returned to Tiruvannamalai she began to see everything — mountains

Arthur Osborne 131

and clouds, trees and flowers — with the eye of a painter, as glorious arrangements of line and colour. Particularly she wanted to make pictures of Arunachala and of our house and garden to send to people. For a start, she decided to paint the garden as seen from our veranda, with the hedge full of flowering cactuses at the end of it and Arunachala rising up behind. Frania had left for an art school in England by this time. She had left some paints behind for her mother to use, but they turned out to be inadequate and some of them dried up. Unwilling to relinquish her project, my wife decided to use oil crayons — she had done one or two attractive crayon paintings in Calcutta. Just when she was starting she got a whitlow on her finger and had to stop. When that was better something else interfered. When the picture finally was completed a rat tore it up at night to make a nest for its young. We took all this as a sign that she should not waste her energies on painting. Housekeeping was not a distraction from meditation; painting was.

This does not mean that I am a Puritan opposed to art and literature. It depends what the alternative is. If the alternative is a superficial or materialistic life, art and literature are an ennoblement of it; but if the alternative is a more direct spiritual effort they are a distraction. At the beginning of a religion (as happened, for instance, in Taoism, Buddhism, Christianity and Islam) art and literature are normally either deprecated or ignored, because the powerful wind that then blows turns men to direct spiritual effort; but when the white heat has cooled down to a coloured glow, art and literature come to be not merely condoned but encouraged as a means of turning men's minds from worldly values to spiritual, leading them gradually through harmonized form to the Formless. Therefore a wealth of religious art arose in these same religions in their mediaeval periods —

132   *My Life and Quest*

the mystic power of Taoist painting and Mahayana sculpture, the Gothic cathedrals of Christendom, the poetry of the Sufi saints and the lace-like arabesques of Islam. For the same reason, various forms of art and literature are not merely encouraged but actually used as techniques of training on some indirect spiritual paths; but on the direct path of Self-enquiry they are a hindrance.

Before I stopped writing I still had two books to edit and one to revise. However, this was work which could be done aloofly; moreover, the editing involved constant preoccupation with the writings and sayings of Bhagavan and was therefore a help and inspiration on the path, not a hindrance. Bhagavan had written little — two prose expositions and two in verse, a few miscellaneous poems and the 'Five Hymns to Arunachala'. All of these had been translated into English and the ashram had published them as separate booklets. Ever since the death of Bhagavan I had been trying to persuade the ashram to put them all together into one volume, so that it would be large enough for booksellers to stock and newspapers to take notice of. Soon after *Buddhism and Christianity* was finished the ashram president told me that they had decided to do so and asked me to edit it. This was published by Riders as *The Collected Works of Ramana Maharshi*, while the ashram also brought out an edition for sale in India.

Apart from the actual writings of Bhagavan, there were various collections of talks with him and of his sayings, the two largest being the 750-page *Talks with Sri Ramana Maharshi* and the two-volume *Day by Day with Bhagavan*. Both of these were in the form of diaries and therefore contained a lot of repetition, with no arrangement according to subject. For the benefit of the general reader I decided that it would be advisable to take passages both from the various recorded talks and the written books and fit them together according to subject. A certain amount of editorial comment was necessary, explaining and connecting the various passages, but it was kept to moderate proportions and printed in a different type so as to be distinguishable at a glance from the words of Bhagavan himself. This book also, entitled *The Teachings of Ramana Maharshi in His Own Words*, was published both by Riders and the ashram.

The only other task remaining was the revision of *The Cosmology of the Stars*, the book I had written in camp on the philosophy underlying astrology. There was really no need to bother with it, but I have a tidy mind and do not like leaving loose ends, so I dug the typescript out of the cupboard where it had been lying. To my surprise I found that it required very little change in substance but had to be completely re-written in order to eliminate the arrogant and aggressive tone that had permeated my style under the influence of Guenon. I sent it to Yorke, but he decided, probably quite rightly, that there would not be sufficient market for such a book, so it remained unpublished.

12

BRIEF ETERNITY

IT WAS ABOUT 6 o'clock one June morning in 1956 that the first awakening to Reality occurred. I was alone in the room when I awoke and sat up in bed. My wife and Frania were sleeping in the next room, and Catherine had already married and left us. I just was — my Self, the beginningless, immutable Self. I had thought 'nothing is changed'. In theory I already understood that it is not anything new; what is eternal cannot be new, what is new cannot be eternal. The only description is what Bhagavan has given: "It is as it is." Only now I experienced it. There was no excitement, no joy or ecstasy, just an immeasurable contentment, the natural state, the wholeness of simple being. There was the thought: "It is impossible ever to be bored". The mind seemed like a dark screen that had shut out true consciousness and was now rolled up and pushed away.

Of course, it is a paradox to speak of the mind being rolled up and at the same time of thoughts coming. Similarly, the mind of the realized man, such as Bhagavan, is said to be dead, but he has thoughts. It seems quite natural when it happens. Perhaps the best explanation would be that the mind as an active centre originating ideas, imagination, plans, worries, hopes and fears ceases to function, but the mind as a mirror condensing pure awareness into thoughts still works.

The thought or feeling that it is impossible ever to be bored may seem banal at such a time, but actually it was fundamental. It is the mind that craves activity and feels bored when it does not get it; the Self is untouched by activity and abides in its pristine state of simple happiness.

From my window at the corner of Park Street I saw the roofs of houses with crows wheeling between them. Again there was a paradox, the feeling that all this was at the same time both real and unreal. This is a paradox that has been much commented on, because it is stressed in Zen teachings. It is what Tennyson was trying to express in a line of 'The Princess' where he says: "And all things were and were not."

I do not know how long the experience lasted. In any case, while it lasted it was timeless and therefore eternal. Imperceptibly the mind closed over again, but less opaque, for a radiant happiness continued. I had my bath and shaved and dressed and then went into the sitting room, where I sat down and held the newspaper up in front of me as though I was reading it, so that no one would see the radiance. I was too vibrant with happiness really to read. The afterglow continued for several weeks, only gradually fading out. Why did I want to hide the radiance? Why did I not shout and dance with joy? I suppose because I have a dour Capricornian temperament beneath the surface exuberance of Sagittarius and am shy of exhibiting any feeling.

At about the same time my wife also had a glimpse of Realization. It was a great help and support to be together on

136

My Life and Quest

the path and often our experiences tallied. Frania also had such a glimpse some eighteen months later. The birth anniversary of Bhagavan falls in late December or early January, varying with the phase of the moon. On this occasion a Tamil devotee living in Calcutta invited us to a celebration on the terraced roof of his house. There must have been about a hundred people gathered there. The previous day there had been a meeting in a public building and speeches had been made, but this evening there was only the singing of religious songs. I could see from the beauty and serenity of Frania's face that she was enjoying exceptionally good meditation; later I learned that it was even more than that. What she described was transparently genuine; and indeed, so little theory did she know that she would have been incapable of expressing it had it not happened.

Afterwards she wrote it down. "I am not the mind nor the body — found myself in the heart; the me that lives after death. There was breath-taking joy in the feeling 'I am', the greatest possible joy, the full enjoyment of existence. No way to describe it — the difference between this joy and complete happiness of the mind is greater than between the blackest misery and the fullest elation of the mind. Gradually — rapidly — my body seemed to be expanding from the heart. It engulfed the whole universe. It didn't feel any more. The only real thing was God (Bhagavan, Arunachala). I couldn't identify myself as any speck in that vastness — nor other people — there was only God, nothing but God. The word 'I' had no meaning any more; it meant the whole universe — everything is God, the only reality."

As this revelation of truth to one so young both in years and in meditation illustrates, a glimpse of Self-realization is not necessarily a token of progress made on the path, at any rate in this lifetime. If it seems bathos to assert that glimpses of the

Arthur Osborne 137

supreme state can occur to people who have no understanding of it and have never sought for it, the answer is that the supreme state is also the natural state, the true state of every man and woman born, if only they knew it; and therefore the wonder is not that it should be occasionally glimpsed but that it should be so widely ignored, that most people should be content, or only vaguely discontent, to go through life circumscribed by the evidence of the physical senses and the rational mind, believing that to be all there is, blind to Reality, blind to their own Self.

There are three possibilities. The first is the occurrence of glimpses of Self-realization to people who have no theoretical knowledge of what it means, that is of the Supreme Identity, who follow no spiritual path, and indeed do not even know that any path or goal exists. Tennyson, to whom I have already referred, was an example of this. He has described it vividly in a private letter: "... a kind of waking trance I have frequently had, right up from boyhood, when I have been all alone. This has generally come upon me through repeating my own name two or three times to myself, silently, till all at once, as it were out of the intensity of consciousness of individuality, the individuality itself seemed to dissolve and fade away into boundless being: and this is not a confused state, but the clearest of the clear, the surest of the sure, the weirdest of the weird, utterly beyond words, where death was an almost laughable impossibility, the loss of personality (if so it were) seeming no extinction, but the only true life... I am ashamed of my feeble description. Have I not said the state is utterly beyond words?"

Actually, the term 'waking trance' is unfortunate because there is nothing trance-like about it. On the contrary it is "the clearest of the clear, the surest of the sure", a realization of pure, indubitable Reality, of one's own true state.

138   *My Life and Quest*

Anthologies of such experiences have been published, and those who wish to can refer to them. It will seem, however, on studying them, that by no means all are glimpses of actual Self-realization. More common are experiences that may be termed intermediate, that is, of Divine Grace or of the supernal wonder of God's creation when seen aright. There is a vast range of such experiences accessible to mystics and to wayfarers on the various paths. However, the traveller on the direct path does not seek them; he seeks only the Self that has the experiences.

The second possibility that I have in mind is the occurrence of a glimpse of Self-realization as an introduction to the path or an encouragement to set forth upon it, as happened with Frania. This also may occur to some one with no previous knowledge, so that the difference from the first possibility mentioned is rather dynamic or functional than static, rather in the effect of the experience than in the experience itself. *The Following Feet* by Ancilla (Longmans) is an account of a life shaped henceforth by such an experience. The experience itself is admirably described:

"It was as if I had moved, in my mind, away from the central place, as if I had always sat on a throne in mid-consciousness, administrating my affairs, and *had stepped down.* It was positive, and I cannot, by taking thought, repeat. It had the stillness of humility shining with surprised joy. . .

"Then, precisely as if that moving off the centre of my own consciousness had set some machinery going, it happened. How can I explain? I can only use negatives.

"I saw nothing, not even light.

"I heard nothing, no voice, no music, nothing.

"Nothing touched me. Nor was I conscious of any Being, visible or invisible.

Arthur Osborne 139

"But suddenly, simply, silently, I was not there. And I was there. It lasted for a moment, yet it was eternal, since there was no time.

"And I knew, as certainly as I know I am trying to write it down, as certainly as I know that I live and eat and walk and sleep, that this world, this universe, is precisely as we see it, hear it, know it, and is at the same time completely different. It is as we see it because we are of it; it is also and at the same time wholly *other*. . .

"But it was not an inkling, it was complete. Yet I do not know in what ways the earth appeared different. It was not different materially. It still had form, and colour, even good and evil, and animals and people, but it was conceived differently, as a whole, perhaps, as a spiritual entity. And it filled me with awe and grave joy and certainty, since I knew for always that it was and no other and that all was well; that it was the answer to all questions. I had no vision of God, or of any person, no vision of Christ, or of any spiritual being. Yet it was all that is, and there was no God, and equally no not-God. It was whole and of the spirit. No words can make it clear. All I can say is that the wholeness seemed akin to that part of me that I should call spirit, as if my spirit were part of it and could not be separated from it.

"How long the experience lasted I have no idea, but I think it was momentary. When it ceased I felt as though I had expended a great deal of time, and that, equally, there was no time in that moment. That timelessness was the clearest impression." (pp. 20-21).

It is noteworthy that, as an after-effect of this experience, she felt precisely as I had when first reading Guenon: "So now I know, and it is all true, and *I have always known it*." This feeling

140   *My Life and Quest*

that one has always known it but did not know that one knew is an important symptom, showing that, even at the very beginning of the path, there is nothing new; the truth is not discovered but recognized.

In a case like this, what I said in an earlier chapter about the alternate manifestation of higher and lower tendencies is apt to apply with peculiar force. The introduction to the path, being so resplendent, is apt to call out all that is best in the person, making him radiant with a new beauty, but, since equipoise is a natural phenomenon, this may be followed by a correspondingly extreme upsurge of his lower tendencies, causing a period of great stress in himself and of distress to those connected with him, before a temporary equilibrium is reached and battle joined between the two forces in him.

The third possibility is that of the seeker in quest of Realization. It was in speaking of this that Bhagavan warned his followers not to expect Self-realization immediately to become permanent, explaining that time and effort are needed to stabilize it and to dissolve the *vasanas* or lower tendencies which drag one back from it even when momentary glimpses appear.

If it seems unjust to the wayfarer that others should receive in apparently unearned largesse that for which he has striven so long without avail, this also is an opportunity for Self-enquiry — who is it that strives unavailingly? Who am I? Despondency itself is an error and therefore an impediment to realization, as I have explained in chapter eight, since it means accepting as real the existence of the unreal, that is, of the apparently unsuccessful ego.

Even looked at from a lower, individual plane, there is no injustice, since no experience of realization can come to one who is not ripe for it, whether the ripeness has been attained

Arthur Osborne 141

in this lifetime or a previous one. When the sun rises, not all buds burst into flower but only those who are ready for flowering. It is no use accusing the sun of injustice. All that one has to concern oneself with is becoming fit and ready. In this, no less than in worldly matters, the injunction of the *Gita* is to be observed: to concern oneself with performing the right action, not with grasping at the reward of the action. Irrespective of visible results, this lifetime should be used for spiritual development, for ripening towards realization of that Ultimate Identity which eternally is, whether realized or not. Indeed, the only real tragedy is a lifetime wasted on meaningless living, not turned to spiritual effort.

A glimpse of Self-realization can be regarded as a breach in the prison-walls of the ego. Its occurrence does not rest with the aspirant; what rests with him is the steady work of erosion, wearing the walls away, until at last they become paper-thin and ready to collapse.

The mind must be completely saturated by understanding of non-duality — that there is only the One Self. It is not enough to hold this as a theory.

Even this mental permeation, however, is only a preliminary, preparing one for the constant practise of Self-enquiry, which will gradually set up the current of awareness. Even though the Sun of Truth has not yet risen, the state of such a man is very different from one who stumbles blindly through the dream of life, taking its appearances for reality, different even from one who awakens occasionally to glimpses of a Reality he does not understand; it is a fuller, more vital, more blessed state, where life, the whole of life, has beauty and significance, and yet, paradoxically, the deprivation of life would be no tragedy, since it is spiritual awareness, not physical life that is the reality. Indeed, that is why the question that any religion teaches about the after-life is relatively unimportant and can interest only philosophers and theologians. Judaism and the original Taoism say nothing on the subject, while Buddha refused to answer questions about it; and therefore scholars gravely argue whether they believed in survival or not. From a spiritual viewpoint, death is not important. "There is no existence of the unreal and no non-existence of the Real", either before death or after. If the ego does not exist now, it does not exist after death either; if an illusory ego seems to exist now it will seem to exist after death also. The thing to do is to strive to awaken to reality now, in this lifetime, and then, as Bhagavan said, death can make no difference; no further change is possible.

13

Retirement

DURING OUR STAY in Calcutta we usually spent the summer holidays at Tiruvannamalai. The journey itself consumed a week, there and back, leaving only about a month to stay there, sometimes less, and at the hottest time of the year; but it was worth it. We appreciated every day of it. Even though the meditation can be continued in any place, there is a vibrant peace at Tiruvannamalai that is immensely invigorating. One holiday we spent at Kalimpong in the Himalayas, but the atmosphere was empty and flaccid in comparison. We visited Shantiniketan in West Bengal, where Tagore had lived and where he founded his university, but felt no living presence.

Altogether we have travelled little and seen few swamis or holy places. As long as the children were at school in the hills we naturally used to spend the hot season with them; and later, when I was working, we were drawn nearly every holiday to Tiruvannamalai. In any case, we had little impetus to travel or

144   *My Life and Quest*

explore. After Bhagavan, who else is there to see? We began to feel the same also about Arunachala.

Not that visits to holy men and holy places are deprecated. They can undoubtedly be beneficial; although, as I said before, the visitor should keep his wits about him and judge carefully whether everything is as holy as it is reputed to be. Only for one who has come under the influence of Bhagavan — indeed, for one who has the right guru — it becomes unnecessary. We met the Dalai Lama when he came as a state guest to Calcutta in 1956. A Bengali publisher had persuaded me to write a simple life of Buddha to be used as a school or college reader. Since the Dalai Lama's visit occurred just when it was finished, we had the idea of asking him to write a brief foreword for it. I was glad that we did, because this gave us the opportunity to meet him, and I found him a person of great beauty. Beneath his charm of manner he made an impression of real power and integrity. We were granted a private interview. He was gracious and interested to know what path we were following. We were not able to explain very successfully, but I presented him with a copy of *Ramana Maharshi and the Path of Self-knowledge* and also left a copy of the little book on Buddha with him. Next day the interpreter gave it back, telling us that it had been read in translation to the Dalai Lama, who had approved of it and written a short foreword stamped with his official seal.

I collected a foreword from the Panchen Lama also, but in him I felt no spiritual presence at all — just a young man in an important position. As soon as I said that the Dalai Lama had written a foreword he said that he would too.

I met the Dalai Lama again in Madras in 1960, when he was touring south India, no longer as a ruling monarch but as a refugee. He looked reduced and rather pathetic, but

Arthur Osborne 145

his charm of manner remained, and there was the same impression of integrity.

Incidentally, the publisher failed to get the Board of Education of any of the states in India to prescribe the book on Buddha for their schools or colleges, despite the foreword, so from a worldly point of view nothing came of the enterprise. I decided that it was not appropriate for me to waste my time and energy on mercenary writing.

Once when we were in Madras, Swami Ramdas came there and visited the house of a friend. My wife went to see him, but I did not. He made a good impression, genial, openhearted, but not the majesty of Bhagavan. He was a simple, childlike person who saw the potential beauty in every one, saw every one as a manifestation of God; and he himself was permanently imbued with the Grace of God. He had many ardent followers, some of them devotees of Bhagavan. One of them, a friend of ours, asked him some years after Bhagavan's death, why he did not stay at Tiruvannamalai, and he replied: "Would you put a candle in the same room with the flaming sun?" I corresponded with him over a sentence in his book _World is God_ (an account of his 1954 world tour) which read like a denial that Bhagavan had disciples, and he explained that he had not intended it to have that meaning; he quite realized that we were Bhagavan's disciples, and indeed owed his illumination to the Grace of Bhagavan. He had meant only that Bhagavan did not give formal initiation. Later he was kind enough to write a foreword to _The Incredible Sai Baba_ for me.

Anandamayi Ma, a famous woman saint of north India, came to Tiruvannamalai a few years after Bhagavan left the body, but we were away in the hills at the time and missed seeing her. She prostrated herself before his tomb, saying: "He is the ocean and we are the rivers that run into it."

146   *My Life and Quest*

During the summer holidays of 1957 I was working on *Buddhism and Christianity in the Light of Hinduism* at Tiruvannamalai and was much impressed by the division of aspirants in the early Buddhist texts into 'non-returners', 'once-returners', 'twice-returners' and so forth, according to whether this was the last incarnation that would be necessary or whether one or more re-births would be needed to complete the *karma* and attain Nirvana. I saw a resemblance to my going back into the world to earn a living and then being drawn home again to Tiruvannamalai, and I found myself frequently repeating: 'May I be a once-returner' in this sense of returning only one more year to Calcutta and then coming to Tiruvannamalai for good, to settle down there. It was only in this sense that I used the phrase, for I should never have willingly considered returning for another incarnation. Indeed, once during an illness in Madras, my vital force seemed to be sinking right down and the last thought that remained in my mind was: 'Let me go or stay, but let me not come back!' Actually, the idea of coming back, the idea that there is any ego to come back and be born again, is a sinking to the exoteric level; it is the same error that I referred to in chapter eight, of ascribing a temporary existence to the unreal and forgetting that 'there is no existence of the unreal and no non-existence of the Real'.

This was not the prayer that I uttered. Indeed, after coming to Bhagavan I never prayed for anything, except sometimes for greater energy and determination on the quest — and that prayer is part of the quest itself. Not that there is anything against prayer in the sense of request. If a man makes physical and mental efforts to attain his desires it is only sensible to make spiritual efforts also. But the man who follows the direct path of Self-enquiry is striving to dissolve the ego that has the desires, so

Arthur Osborne 147

how can he at the same time pray to gratify them? It would be contradictory, going against his own efforts, however high or unselfish the desires may seem to be. He simply lets things come as they will, asking to whom it is that they come.

Even the path of devotion and submission leaves no place for prayer in the sense of petition if it is as wholehearted as Bhagavan demanded. Asking is not submitting. If one is totally submitted to the Will of God, the only prayer that remains is 'Thy Will be done'. And since one knows that God's Will is always done, whether one prays for it or not, even that becomes redundant. All one can say is: "I surrender my self to You; do as You like with it." And beyond even that comes the attitude: "There is nothing to surrender. All this is Yours. I surrender only the false idea I had that it was mine." But, as with art and literature, it is a question of what is the alternative. If the alternative is reliance on the ego, or on chance or worldly influence or other people, then prayer is better. It is only fair to add that there are plenty of devotees of Bhagavan who do pray to him and that their prayers are answered.

My frequent repetition 'May I be a once-returner' certainly came very near to being a prayer, even though it was not formally so, and was not so intended. When we got back to Calcutta I had the constant feeling that our stay there was not for long, though it was impossible to envisage how the change could come about. Then, less than a month before the next summer holiday, it was as though Bhagavan picked up the kaleidoscope and shook it and all the pieces fell into shape. Adam got a place at a university, with a grant to cover his expenses; Frania passed her Senior Cambridge and left school, deciding that she did not want to go on to college; my health deteriorated, making professional life more difficult; the school paid me a bonus as

148 My Life and Quest

well as my provident fund; it was arranged that several newspapers would send to me at Tiruvannamalai books for review — suddenly retirement had become possible.

My whole professional life had been unsatisfactory, with frequent changes and insecurity, which was but a natural repercussion of my rejection of security and status when at Oxford; and yet I was now enabled to retire at 51, when many more successful men, in the worldly sense of success, had years of professional work still before them.

In April 1958 we packed up and left Calcutta for good. We thought we knew hardly any one there, but our compartment was full of flowers when the train pulled out, and there was a farewell crowd on the platform. That was on the 12th April; when we drew up in Madras on the morning of the 14th we found the station beflagged and a festive air everywhere, as though in greeting; and we were told that April 14th was Tamil New Year's Day. We stayed with friends and spent the night in Madras, leaving on the evening of the 15th and arriving early next morning in Tiruvannamalai. At the ashram also we found festivity, as though for our arrival. It turned out that the anniversary of Bhagavan's leaving the body (originally on 14th April but varying with the phases of the moon, like the Western Easter) fell on the 16th that year. In such ways we were made to see that the homecoming was auspicious. When people began to ask, as usual, how soon we had to go back, we were able to answer, "Not at all."

At last we had come home. No place had been our home before this. We had been spiritual wayfarers, and this state had been reflected in a nomadic life on earth. Gdynia, Bangkok, Madras, Calcutta, all seemed mere temporary camping places; in none of them had we struck roots and felt at home. Even our

Arthur Osborne 149

previous stay at Tiruvannamalai had had a temporary atmosphere about it, partly from the knowledge that we should have to go out into the world again to a professional life, and partly because of the difficulty of finding permanent accommodation before our own house was built, so that we had three abodes in less than three years. We had had a close family life, but now two of our children were gone out into the world and the third was soon to follow. We had made a few friends, formed no attachments: for the wayfarer there can only be companionship with fellow pilgrims upon the path, and they are few.

Retirement did not mean a life of hobbies and gentle pottering, but only of a more complete dedication, more constant effort. Indeed, it is dangerous for one on the quest to retire from life in the world too early. If the mind is not yet capable of holding daylong to the quest, it is better for it to have some surface activity such as professional work; failing this, it will find relief in trivialities, day-dreaming, imagination or erudition or fall into some false kind of half-sleep, half-trance; in some way its keenness will be impaired. Bhagavan was gracious to us. My wife was able to divide the day between housework and meditation, while I found occupation in my book reviewing and in editing the *Collected Works* and *The Teachings*. Gradually, as such occupations dwindled, isolated days began to appear, or even a whole week, when there was no outer activity for the mind and I found it possible most of the time to remain poised in the current of awareness, conscious of outer things but with the mind almost inactive, neither fretting at its inactivity nor plunging into trivialities or forced activity. Nevertheless it was a constant effort at first and was very tiring.

Apart from our own *sadhana* or spiritual efforts, we found in another way also that it was good that we should be here —

150   *My Life and Quest*

so many visitors come to Tiruvannamalai, many of them for the first time, from many different countries, and they expect to find a few people resident here who can tell them about Bhagavan and explain his teaching. Many made friends with us or stayed with us here. They wrote about their desire to return. Even when that was not possible, the visit often marked a stage on their path.

About two years after my retirement I began for the first time to see my whole past life quite objectively, as though it concerned some other person or some previous incarnation. Not only that, but it took form in my mind, word for word, just as I would tell it to some one if the need arose, and going right back to infancy. This was an asset on the quest, revealing much that had hitherto remained obscure; nevertheless it began to occupy my mind so much as to interfere with meditation. Was I to go back on my determination to write no more books? There it was, already written in my head; and it was not the sort of book on some subject which I had renounced. It was, though not in the sense I had envisaged, a book about the quest itself. I repeatedly turned away from it, but it did not disappear from my mind. (Then I remembered what Bhagavan had said about one of the *Five Hymns to Arunachala*, that the words of the beginning of it rose up before him and, even though he dismissed them, saying 'What have I to do with these words?', they kept coming back till he wrote them down). Was it a book that had to get written? In order to see, I wrote out the first chapter, scarcely stopping to think, just word for word, as it was in my mind. Immediately my thoughts left that period of my life, not even coming back to it, but concentrating on the next. So I wrote out the next too, and thus chapter-by-chapter till I had written the whole book, which I thought was here ended. (I must admit, though, that I afterwards worked for nearly a year on its revision and amplification.) Still the question of publication remained — whether it was legitimate to inflict my personal life on others. I worked on it for a couple of years more, cutting out here and adding there, until what finally remained was indeed a story of the quest. And by that time I had discovered that the book was not ended but had further chapters.

14

Continued Quest

OF COURSE, the book was not ended, because the quest still continued. Progress was still in waves. They were more visible now and followed one another more closely, while the troughs between them were shorter and less deep and gloomy. Nevertheless, any trough at all had become intolerable. Even a day or a part of a day deprived of the current of awareness was like being thrust down into an underground cell with no sunlight or fresh air, no freedom of movement. The time had come when the very concept of any other mode of life was unthinkable.

After about three years a series of great waves started, each one beginning at the crest and gradually subsiding into a level stretch, when it was necessary to cling to it tenaciously till the next wave arose. Each constituted a new mode of approach, one might almost say a new revelation, not to be lost in the end but rather absorbed as another strand in the totality of meditation. Such stages are not merely successive but can be progressive also.

153

The account that follows was written piece by piece, like a diary, and therefore the perspective changes to some extent as the path ascends higher up the mountainside.

First came a wave of concentration on pure being. Bhagavan had said that what is necessary is not to be conscious of being a man or woman or a father or son or a businessman or office-goer, but simply to BE; and now, like floodgates opened over arid land, it was suddenly easy. It happened naturally, without effort. How can there be effort to be oneself? One cannot do other than slipping off unobserved into thought or bringing up some urgent problem which would not be in the least urgent if one had a visitor to talk to or a book to read, or simply feeling sleepy. The only way is to persevere.

With persistence the mind can be both strengthened and disciplined in this way and its intuitive powers developed.

This practise of self-awareness is close to the Buddhist practise of mindfulness. Whatever you are doing, be mindful of doing it. When you shave, shave: don't speculate what letters will come with the morning post. When you eat, eat; don't read the paper or chatter while doing so.

These two exercises are not alternatives to Self-enquiry but can supplement it. If Self-enquiry is a concentrated effort when you are alone, morning and evening, these can be practised unobserved at any time.

To return to my story: some weeks later, when the power of this meditation had waned, I woke up slowly one morning; to be more precise, consciousness returned without being focused at once on the 'I'-thought. The dream-sequence just left behind was seen on one side and the waking sequence soon to come on the other.

One cannot be other than oneself. Only one's restless thoughts entangle being in a cocoon of multiform anxiety. Now,

154 *My Life and Quest*

quite suddenly, but with gradually diminishing force and clarity over the ensuing weeks, it was possible to feel the simple being, the simple I-am-ness. There was no need to sit in a fixed posture for it; it could be evoked, or came spontaneously without evocation, at any time, while sitting, walking, even talking, while getting breakfast in the morning or tea in the afternoon (because I took over these lighter chores). My day began with meditation from five to six in the morning, and then I got up, had my bath, pottered about the garden till seven and then got breakfast. From eight till nearly nine I sat in meditation at the ashram during the chanting of the *Vedas*, then waited there for the post, which came between nine and half past.

As explained in chapter ten, man has three states or functions — action, thought and being; and of these being is obviously the essential, since he cannot act or think unless he first is, whereas he always is whether he thinks and acts or not — for instance, in deep sleep. And yet thought and action so cover over being that he is usually unaware of it.

Let me add here, in parenthesis, that awareness of being is a very useful spiritual exercise that can be practised daily. Sitting in your armchair or on a bus seat, or standing in a queue, just be aware of yourself. There is no need to close your eyes, because the environment also can be noticed, no need for strain or tension; indeed, it is an exercise rather in relaxation than concentration. There is only one condition: that the mind should not be allowed to wander away from this awareness into any train of thought. For instance, you can see the clock on the shelf and hear it ticking, but not think that you paid too much for it or wonder whether Aunt Jane will like it or whether you forgot to wind it up. If some more definite focus for the attention is needed, the most suitable is your own

Arthur Osborne 155

breathing; not trying to regulate it or force it into any pattern, just watching it.

Simple as this exercise is, it may not be easy at first, because the mind is as restless as a monkey and resists quiet in every way it can, like floating on the surface of consciousness without affecting it. Bhagavan had said that the state to be aimed at is a sort of waking sleep; also that it can be experienced at the moment between waking and sleeping. I prolonged the state as long as possible. During the weeks that followed, this formed my mode of meditation: particularly, of course, while waking from sleep (while falling asleep I found it more difficult) but also throughout the day — retiring into impersonal consciousness, seeing the flow of events drift past on its surface. Paradoxically, this state of 'sleep' is also the true waking state — 'sleep' because untroubled by differentiation (although in consciousness, not, like physical sleep, in darkness); 'waking' because truly aware, despite the twofold veil of illusion, that of dreams of night and that of apparent waking world by day.

Some weeks later, this meditation also had lost its vigour and one morning, soon after waking, an old *vasana* asserted itself. It is said that the last to go is the sexual urge. Angry and disappointed at this resurgence of a *vasana*, I turned to Self-enquiry: "There can't be a *vasana* unless there is some one to have it. Who is it that has this *vasana*? Who am I?"

This time, however, the use of Self-enquiry as a weapon proved unnecessary. When at 8 o'clock that morning I sat down as usual before the tomb of Bhagavan at the ashram to meditate during the chanting of the *Vedas*, the thought came: "Why occupy your mind with physical union when you can turn it to the universal spiritual union?" Therewith a flood of Grace swept over me, setting up a meditation on all things going out from the

156   *My Life and Quest*

One, as a man's breath spreads out when he exhales in frosty air, and at the same time yearning back towards unity in the One.

Thought? Meditation? What word can one find to describe an inner certitude which is not clearly defined like a theory and which is so far from being merely mental that it carries with it a wave of joy and a tingling of the body reaching to the very toes and fingertips? Not 'realization', because it seems best to reserve that for the supreme state of realized unity. When modern philosophers pride themselves on having progressed beyond the saints and philosophers of earlier times who put faith above reason, they are misunderstanding the meaning of the word 'faith'. They regard it as simply believing something is true because one has been told so, whereas, at least in some cases, it must be referring to an inner certitude such as I am trying to describe, which really is beyond reason.

Even as this meditation started I appreciated, despite its magnificence, that it was on a lower level than Self-enquiry or the two previous approaches, since it presumed the existence of 'all this'. Nevertheless, I told myself, it was useful because it supplied the element of *prem* (love) and *ananda* (bliss), which had hitherto been rather lacking in my *sadhana*. Also it served the immediate purpose of dissolving the sexual urge. Just as, at an earlier stage of *sadhana*, the desire to smoke had vanished as soon as the true substitute for it appeared, so now with this.

If any one should ask why this meditation on unity should be presumed 'right' and dwelling on physical union 'wrong', the answer is simple: on the spiritual path whatever hardens and exaggerates the illusion of a separate individual being is harmful, whatever weakens or dissolves it is beneficial.

The second great command of Judaeism and Christianity — to love your neighbour as yourself — is a corollary of the first — to

Arthur Osborne 157

love God wholeheartedly; because it is only when you yearn towards the One and see all beings equally as emanations from or manifestations of the One that equal love flows out to them.

There is tremendous wealth and power in the meditation on unity. All the events of your life, and those still to be enacted, all the people you have known, yourself among them, all the epochs of history, the eons of the geologist, the inscrutable worlds of the astronomer, all expanding from the focal point within you. And all this is no dull, earthy union but an incandescent white flame. Powers and experiences could probably be achieved this way; to one in whose nature it was they might come unsought. It is better to avoid them.

This continued to be my *sadhana* for some weeks, and then towards morning one night I repeatedly woke or half woke from sleep, reminding myself that I must pull my mind away from the current of dreams it was pursuing and fix it in meditation. On finally awakening, I saw that the same applied to the daytime sequence of events also. All this, including thinking about it, writing about it, trying to awake from it, is a current of dreams. One has to renounce it and fix the mind in meditation. This now became my mode of approach.

It is a wonderful weapon against distracting thoughts and against any regret or desire — not wanting to change the course of the dream but simply to wake up from it.

The Self which I am is dreaming me — the individual me — and all this world, as well as other individuals and their worlds. (That is the meaning of the story of Krishna embracing at the same time every one of his 16,000 wives, each in her own room of the palace.) Therefore what has to be done is to submit, take life as it comes, let things happen, while at the same time striving to wake up from it all. As long as it is taken

158 — *My Life and Quest*

to be real, the dream cannot be recognized as one and therefore there is no awakening.

In fact the one thing necessary is to eliminate by any and every means the sense of being an individual entity. Gradually over the course of two days the attempt to wake up changed this. There is consciousness but not a me who is conscious; there is action but no one who acts.

The mind is like a mill grinding the thoughts that we constantly feed into it in an unbroken though ever-changing flow, like the stream-of-consciousness type of novel that James Joyce originated. It doesn't care whether grave or trivial so long as it is kept constantly supplied. And at night, in dreams, it chews over the cud of what was supplied to it by day. Nearly all this activity is wasted energy. It prevents concentration and does not really clarify one's mind. And all of it is based on the very assumption one is trying to destroy, of an individual being who decides and acts. So I began instead to suspend thought, refusing to feed anything into the mill, retaining only pure consciousness — and, of course, observation of things happening. The mind was allowed to deal with anything requiring thought as and when it arose, but not to prefigure it before it arose or re-enact it after it was finished. I was surprised how simple and what a relief this was and wondered why I had not started doing it systematically long before; and then it occurred to me that without a good deal of previous meditation it would not have been feasible. Until it has been brought well under control the mind abhors a vacuum. Even now this practise proved far from easy once the surge of Grace that always accompanied a new approach had passed. On the other hand, it began to occur spontaneously without effort.

And the result? Not boredom, as some might suppose. Boredom is in the mind, in fact is the mind's defence against

Arthur Osborne 159

anything approaching a vacuum. Rather there was an immense euphoria. Not any sort of vision or experience, for that would imply the duality of knower and known, or, more correctly, the triplicity of seer, sight and seen, whereas pure consciousness is the unity beyond this. The flow of idle, ceaseless thoughts is as much a hindrance to meditation as are attachments; in this way it is stilled.

The mind by nature is feminine, that is, passive and receptive; instead it makes itself masculine, imagining itself to be originating and creating. In doing so it postulates a fictitious ego. It becomes so busy and so persistently turned out towards its imaginary creations that it makes itself oblivious to the higher perceptions it should receive. The task is to turn it right again, from creating a mirage, to receiving impressions of reality.

It is very hard for the mind to understand that it has to do nothing to attain Realization; in fact it is itself the hindrance and has only to stop interfering. That is why Bhagavan said that you have only to disrealize unreality and Reality will be realized. It is the mind that creates the unreality. The *Quran* repeatedly enjoins not to make mischief in the land, and the *Tao Te Ching* says that the less the emperor governs, the happier and more prosperous the people are. The meaning is the same: the mind is the emperor or the mischief-maker; it has only to keep quiet and one's nature, the empire, will develop in all its pristine purity.

The purpose of meditation is to steady the mind and prevent it jumping and chattering like a monkey by holding it to one thought. If you suspend its activity without the one thought that is still better. If it becomes too restive the best way of controlling it is either by an act of Self-enquiry, turning steadily to see whether it really exists or not, and what it is that exists, or by an act of faith and submission, resigning yourself to keep

160 *My Life and Quest*

still and let the Unknown take charge. That is what Christ meant by laying down one's life for His sake. He who lays down his conscious mind for Christ's sake, for the Spirit, the Unknown, will find it; but also he who clings to it, seeking to preserve it, will lose it.

This approach continued for over eight weeks and was then replaced by humdrum, pedestrian, but very necessary technique introduced not by a new surge of Grace, as previous ones had been, but by a dream.

I dreamed that Bhagavan came to the house for me, but as I was leaving with him I saw a low fire burning on the drive outside and understood that I must first put it out for fear that the strong wind that was blowing might carry sparks to the house and start a conflagration. The fire, of course, was the ego, made up of *vasanas* — desires, interests, attachments. The dream might be called satisfactory insofar as it was only embers, not a blaze, and not in the house but outside; however I felt it dismal that there should still be a fire to put out at all.

Thereupon I started a straight fight with *vasanas*, or, I hoped, a mopping-up operation — hunting them out of their hide-outs and setting on them — any desires or attractions, any thoughts, however slight, of what would happen (since the future exists as definitely as the past), any dwelling on books I had read — a state of constant vigilance. The heathen were weak and scattered when the Israelites conquered the Holy Land, but they should have been exterminated; because they were not they grew strong and became a menace later — an excellent allegory of the remaining *vasanas*; they were the embers which might spark a fire.

This was in November 1961. The previous winter I had suffered from a severe bronchial infection leading to suffusion

Arthur Osborne 161

of the lungs and suffocating attacks, and for a while recovery was considered doubtful. It was cured through my wife's homoeopathic treatment but there was continued shortness of breath and liability to a relapse. At this time a relapse did occur — perhaps due to my carelessness in continuing to sleep with open windows once the cool night winds had set in. Anyway, giving no thought to the outcome was a good opportunity for the attack on *vasanas*.

From renunciation of *vasanas* to abnegation of the ego that has them. Then what remains? Only the experience of being, with the mind as a servant registering impressions, not an independent being reliving the past or anticipating the future. But it required continuous effort and alertness to retain this state. Particularly was this so now, because there was no new surging of Grace, while the vitality was lowered by sickness and the whole day was free for the task — no books came for review, no work of any kind, and I was not well enough to lend a hand in the house or garden. For three days old *vasanas* rose up again, such as I had believed long dead — even regret for my youthful folly and for the loss of an Oxford career.

The next day I was able to go to the ashram again for the first time since my illness. Entering the old hall, where I had sat so often before Bhagavan, I sat down in the same place before his couch, on which his full length portrait now rested, and waited for an answer, puzzled and dejected by this new counter-attack but determined not to give in to it. The thought arose in my mind as an answer: "This is like the assault of the old *vasanas* upon Buddha during his night of vigil under the bodhi-tree before his final Awakening."

With some clear understanding of the meaning I felt better. Physically my cough was clearing out old deposits from

162

My Life and Quest

the lungs; spiritually old *vasanas* were being cleared out from the mind.

I found that it was equally possible to maintain impersonal awareness or to let the mind display its magic box of tricks. There was attraction both ways, but it was possible to choose awareness and hold it.

No new approach came. None was needed now that simple being, impersonal awareness, was possible. It became a straight fight with thoughts. Some, the powerful, emotion-laden ones, would crash through the hedge and have to be met head-on and driven back; others, more subtle, would wriggle in like serpents and get a grip before they could be observed. It was a ding-dong battle. Day and night it went on. At night the defences are weakened, and I would wake up and catch the mind rambling through a useless sequence of dreams — there is the clear, vivid, symbolical dream that can be a useful indicator of one's state, but there is also the endless, worthless, confused dream sequence which merely picturises the daytime thoughts and impulses. It was this that I was at war with. I would wake up and pull the mind back to quiet. It might be necessary to sit up in meditation for awhile to clear out the rubbish. With effort, control was established and the dream rambling stopped. By daytime also the revolt of the *vasanas* died down.

Sat-Chit-Ananda the true state is called — Being-Consciousness-Bliss. Ultimately they fuse into One; in fact they are three aspects of the same. There was already the experience of being and the impersonal awareness, but not the bliss which should draw the mind of its own volition to this state and make it abide there effortlessly, over-riding any counter-attraction that might seek to draw it outwards.

There are cases, on a devotional and ecstatic path, where the aspect of bliss develops first. Despite the intense joy, this is

Arthur Osborne 163

more dangerous and less satisfactory. The times of joy are interspersed with periods of black misery when the Face of the Beloved is veiled; moreover the violent alternation and passionate longing may induce irrational behaviour or even over-balance the mind. Therefore, for instance, it is a dictum of the Sufi masters that the path of sobriety is preferable to that of inebriation. Even so powerful a master as Ramakrishna was thought mad when he first became immersed in ecstasy.

At this stage I had a sudden impulse to be afraid and draw back. This is a temptation which must be unhesitatingly cast aside or it may vitiate a lifetime's striving. It is as though a man were to toil through dense forest and craggy mountain, in hardship and frequent danger, seeking the heavenly city, and then, when its outer ramparts at last loom up, separated from him only by a narrow chasm, were to turn aside, fearing to jump. Henceforth he sits listlessly by the wayside or wanders without aim, unable to return to the state of spiritual ignorance from which he started but without initiative to press forward. There are many such derelicts.

> There is a tide in the affairs of men,
> Which, taken at the flood, leads on to fortune;
> Omitted, all the voyage of their life
> Is bound in shallows and in miseries.
> On such a full sea we are now afloat;
> And we must take the current when it serves,
> Or lose our venture.
> — Shakespeare, *Julius Caesar,* act 4, scene 3

However, it should be added that this depressing prospect (like I said twice before in this book about the many who are called but not chosen) is depressing only from the narrow viewpoint of this lifetime. Actually, a man's whole course or life-

164   *My Life and Quest*

sequence is a journey leading through however many twists and turns, ravines and bare hillsides, marshy jungles and thirsty plains, to the goal of supreme bliss that is his true nature. It is a pilgrimage lasting many days, each day being one lifetime. A whole day may be wasted; a man may scramble down the hillside after gleaming berries that turn out sour or poisonous when plucked, or he may play around and reach no shelter by nightfall. But the path remains, ineluctable. He has only made the next day's journey more arduous.

The discovery that life is a pilgrimage, that it has a goal and therefore a meaning, is an immense blessing, but it does not necessarily mean that the goal will be attained in this lifetime. The number of days still required would depend partly on the distance from the goal, partly on the energy with which the pilgrim presses forward. Such advance as he does make is not wasted, even though he grows tired and relaxes his efforts before the end of the day. He will wake up so much further forward for the next day's journey. This is expressly guaranteed in the *Bhagavad Gita*: "He who fell from yoga is born (again) in a pure and fortunate house. Or he even comes into a family of wise yogis, though a birth such as this is very hard to obtain in this world. There he obtains the buddhic attainments of his previous incarnations, and thence he again strives for full accomplishment" (Ch. 6, v. 40-43, trans. Ernest Wood).

But what of the objections of Christian and Muslim readers who say they do not believe in reincarnation but in an afterlife of heaven or hell? 'Believe in' is such an unsatisfactory term; it is better to understand. There is indeed an afterlife of heaven or hell, on the relative plane, as Buddhism and Hinduism also teach. All this is as real as you are to yourself, Bhagavan said in reply to a question. This is the state in which the soul reaps the good or

Arthur Osborne 165

evil karma which it has laid up for itself in the life on earth. But after this has been exhausted it comes back to continue its course, to make new karma, good or bad, in a new life, starting at the level to which it had arisen or sunk in its previous life.

For one who has intuitively understood the ultimate truth of Oneness it is not a matter of belief or even argument; it follows naturally that the ultimate and eternal state cannot be a state of multiplicity and diversity. 'In the beginning there was God alone.' On that they agree. That is the eternal reality. Apart from that, whatever is called into being had a beginning and is therefore not eternal. Whatever had a beginning must have an end, be it heaven, earth or hell. It is that end, attained consciously and therefore in pure Beatitude, which is the goal towards which the pilgrim strives. If any say that they do not want to attain it because it means giving up their individuality, they have Christ's blunt reply; that he who clings to his life will lose it. And in any case, what they are clinging to is an illusion, and an illusion is not eternal. Sooner or later, if not in this lifetime, they will understand. But they may create much suffering for themselves on the way. Modern Christian writers have argued a lot from an anthropomorphic level about what they call 'the question of suffering'. It is indeed unanswerable from this level, where a venerable old man called God is supposed to send his children out on to earth for a few years, for no apparent purpose, and then call them back and reward or punish them endlessly, century after century, millennium after millennium, aeon after aeon, through and beyond all recordable time, for the way they behaved there. At least, one would say, he might let them be happy during their brief moment of fate-creating life. But from a higher viewpoint the question fades out and ceases to exist. Since life has a purpose, the attainment of the supreme goal, the measuring

166

rod is not the amount of enjoyment obtained or of pain avoided but the distance travelled towards the goal or away from it, that is to say the development of favourable or unfavourable latent qualities, leaving man in a better or worse state than before. The real gauge of success or failure in life is the state in which a man is when his time comes to leave it. Obviously, going against the purpose of life, which means against one's own true nature, causes suffering. Following it removes suffering. One does not find the saints in any religion complaining of suffering; in fact their most obvious common characteristic is happiness and contentment, even though afflicted by sickness or poverty or other apparent ills. Nor is the egoist truly happy, though his circumstances may appear fortunate. The four basic truths on which Buddhism is based go straight to the heart of the matter. There is suffering (the state of spiritual ignorance). There is a cause for suffering (clinging to ephemeral and apparent reality and ignoring the purpose of life). There is relief from suffering (by relinquishing the unreal and turning to the Real). And there is a way to attain this relief (the Quest).

One last explanation to remove another barrier that theorists unnecessarily raise up against one another. How does this doctrine of a path trod over many lifetimes accord with the Buddhist doctrine of *anatta,* that there is no ego to experience heaven or hell or to be reborn or tread the path? Hindu teachers say the same. When Bhagavan was asked about rebirth he would be quite likely to answer: "First find out whether you are born now." The whole point of Self-enquiry is to break through the apparent reality of the ego to its true unreality. 'There is no existence of the unreal and no non-existence of the Real.' Therefore the realized man does not go to heaven at death and is reborn on earth; he just is. However, for one who has not

Arthur Osborne 167

realized the Self an illusory ego appears to exist in this life and therefore appears to survive it and follow stage after stage of the path. It may be good to remember in theory that this is only an appearance, but what is needed is to realize it.

And now to return to my story. In order to safeguard against any traces of hesitance, I began to practise dying — that is being in readiness to lay down life or the mind completely. There must be no stipulation that perception of a body and world should be restored again after dying, because that would be bargaining, not surrender. If they are restored, all right; if not, all right. You are not ready to wake up from a dream if you stipulate that you should still watch its course, like a cinema, after waking; if you do, all right; if it vanishes into wakefulness, all right.

Also the readiness to die must not be because life is sour or oppressive or futile. That — the suicide's attitude — carries with it the obverse, that if conditions were changed and made attractive you would cling to life. That is not surrender but rebellious rejection of the terms of life offered to you.

I had the feeling: "I am ready to give up my life but it is not accepted. What am I to do now?" The whole day it continued, and so poignant that the thought kept coming: "This is a theme for a poem. What a pity I'm not a poet." The next day too the same feeling continued, and the same thought about the poem. In the evening I was compelled to write it and found to my surprise that it was a poem. Indeed, the second verse was so poignant that I could not read it through without tears coming.

From then on the book continued in the form of poems. I never knew in advance what they would be about. Indeed, I sometimes prepared a list of themes that I wanted to write about, but when a poem came it might be on something quite different. Nevertheless, they continued, though in an indirect way, to be a record of the quest and therefore, although each one is a separate poem and can be read by itself, if read together it should be consecutively — for instance, it would not make sense to read the first after the second, or either of them after the third. The third is an example of an important phenomenon — that some of them described a state not yet permanently mastered. I felt some hesitation at first as to whether it was sincere to write such poems, but they came and demanded to be written; and later on fragments of them would constantly recur to me, like a *mantram*, and were a means of help on the path. Perhaps they will be to others also.

I never knew when they would come and in what form. It was quite irregular. For instance, 'Waking and Sleeping' took about two weeks to write; a fragment, perhaps no more than a line and a half, coming one day and then, after several days' interval, another fragment. On the other hand, 'The Expanse' and 'Be Still' were both written the same day.

After the first few poems, I found that they tended to be either blank verse or regular rhymed lyrics, the more philosophical being blank verse and the more intuitive lyrics. The outer difference between poetry and prose being that poetry is formal and disciplined language and prose comparatively informal and undisciplined, it seems to me unnatural to write formless poetry. If it is not going to conform to the discipline of verse, let it be prose.

Or
Silence.

POEMS

A Testament

Poem

This believe: I tell you what I know
From own experience; nothing of hearsay;
What I have tried and proved and found it so,
Following a guide, a Master of the Way.

Section One

But first what sense-perception tells us all.
The world in endless vista trails away
Into a past remote beyond recall.
Endlessly too the future looms ahead.
Between the two your pin-point life-days fall,
From the being born up to the being dead.
And then the ripples that you caused subside;
Another holds your office, sleeps in your bed,
While Life moves on with unperturbed stride,
As though you had not been. Even while you are,
Nothing is there secure, little for pride.
Health is on loan from time; frustrations mar
Ambition and achievement; friendships end
In death or forgetting. From afar
Old age creeps on, filching the zest you lend
To work and pleasure, chilling the vital power,
Still narrowing the circle you defend
Of life's attachments, till the final hour
When thoughts, drawn in from schemes for which you fought,
From work you lived for, office held or power,
From wife and friend, from child, things sold and bought,

172

Converge on one point only, your next breath;
Stripped of attachment, to naked being brought,
To be squeezed out through the narrow womb of death.

Section Two

So far goes sight; so far men agree;
But probing into what comes after death
Their views diverge. Varied but mainly three
The stands they take.

                  Some there are who hold
Death is the end: nothing again to be,
Nothing to know; for all your tale is told,
And that poor thing that rots in the dark ground
Is all that is of the once manifold
Lover of fair faces and sweet sound
That trod the earth and thought that he was you.
Others there are who see life girdled round
With brighter spheres of forms forever new,
As much more vivid than the earth-forms here
As peacock's throat than sparrow's dingy hue.
There (a spaceless 'there' as dreams appear)
Forces bred up on earth but out of sight—
Courage that goes straight on in spite of fear,
Or twisted guilt submerged from the clear light
Of conscious mind—rise and surround a man
In outer forms of terror or delight;
His own brood, hidden for the earth-life span,
Now torturing his disembodied soul
Eternally if evil; but for who ran
Life's race on earth to the appointed goal
Peace everlasting, bliss past words to tell.

Others declare that this is not the whole.
One season's harvest can't forever sell,
Or one life's balance, whether good or bad,
Consign eternally to heaven or hell.
Man's inner life materialises, clad
In incorporeal forms, they too admit;
But thus the reckoning, whether glad or sad,
Is closed, books balanced: there's an end of it.
Thence he returns once more to life on earth,
At that same level he himself made fit
By use or misuse of his former birth:
Free once again to rise, or free to sink,
The architect again of his own worth.
Again the bell tolls; again the brink
Of death is crossed to living more intense,
More heaven or hell, than earth-bound mind can think.
Thus a man's life brings on its recompense,
Rising before him. Inexorably the Wheel
Swings round from growth to harvest, from the dense
Earth-life that builds to regions that reveal
What there he built. And thus from life to life
Can man increase in stature, till he feel
A brimming joy in what before was strife
And no more yearn to earth-ways, no more cling
To memory or desire, as with a knife
Cut off all craving. Nothing again can bring
Rebirth or grief or death to such a one,
Free as the stars, free as the winds that sing
His glory on the hill-tops, beyond the sun,
In his own radiance gloriously bedight,
Absorbed unending in the Unbegun,
Beyond the parting of the day and night,
Changeless, he sees the changing world aright.

SECTION THREE

Not equally at fault these views. The first
Alone is wholly wrong. The next contains
All that man needs of truth to be well versed
In his own interest, and from petty gains
Followed by great loss to turn and seek
His heritage of bliss, purchased by pains
Prepaid but transient, in prospect bleak,
Like Muslim's dower for his unseen bride,
In retrospect nothing of which to speak.
The third view also can as well provide
Incentive and a way—all that men need.

Yet these three views of man, however wide
They move apart, all spring from the same seed
Of error, for they all alike declare
You are that sentient body whence proceed
Cravings like roots, like branches in the air
Thoughts and ideals; hedged by necessity.
Mere fantasy! No such thing is there!
You are pure Consciousness, Eternity,
Wherein birth, death and world are but such stuff
As dreams are made on. No hyperbole!
Just as a night-time dream seems real enough,
So long as it lasts, within your mortal mind,
So your life's journey, whether smooth or rough—
Between deep hedgerows fragrantly entwined
With honeysuckle, all the air athrob
With singing of the birds, your steps combined
With those of loved companion, such as rob
Exhaustion of its pain, night of its fears,
Or over arid crags, where not to sob

For weariness were hard when the sun sears
And only thorn-trees cast a stunted shade,
While all ahead the naked shale appears—
All that same dream-stuff out of which is made
You mortal self. All that is known or seen,
With you in it, a pageant is, displayed
Harmless in you, like pictures on a screen.

Awake! For dawn has set the sky aflame!
Awake from dreaming what has never been
To find the universe entire a game
Forever changed, you evermore the same.

Section Four

This does not mean there are two selves in you,
One universal and the other bound
By name and form, a transient being who
From birth to death treads out his little round.
Rather amnesia. One born rich and great,
Pre-eminent over all around,
Forgets his own identity, so fate
Leads him to some factory that is his,
Did he but know, to queue up at the gate,
Imploring work. Only one self he is,
Yet twofold: so long as he forgets—
A life of labour and indignities;
Remember, and fate instantly resets
Life as it was before misfortune's drag.
Or that poor knight who, fallen in folly's nets
Travelled Spain's dusty roads on a lean nag,
Windmills for foes, delusion for a flag.

Section Five

How, from pure Consciousness quite unalloyed,
Unfettered being, unimpeded Bliss,
Was that high equilibrium destroyed
and your eternal state brought down to this?
And why? Such questions not at all contribute
To man's awaking. Nought that is amiss
Can they set right. Every such dispute
Is useless, but not harmless; it misleads,
Lending this seeming world the attribute
Of real being, of something that proceeds
In course of time from that eternal state
That was before. Thus ignorantly it pleads
The cause of ignorance. In truth time's spate
Of endless forms is no more than a dream,
While That-which-was remains. Early and late,
Time and the world, are shadow shows that seem
True being only to the clouded mind.

One question only is a worthy theme:
How to dissolve the subtle mists that blind,
What the entangled aspirant can do
To break the Lilliputian threads that bind.
Therefore I write to point a pathway through
The maze of fancied being to the true.

Section Six

First, understanding—not philosophy,
For truth is simple; thought like a playful cat
With skein of wool tangles it wilfully—
Simply that Being is and you are That.

Therefore to know the essential self of you
Is to know all; but not by gazing at,
As one can know another, for Not-Two
The Ultimate. Knowing in that high sense
Is simple being. Being alone is true.

If understanding fails or can dispense
Only a murky glow, as from a lamp
That smokes and flickers in the wind, defence
From weakness, fortitude alone to tramp
The pilgrim way, can come from faith—not blind
But bearing deep experience's stamp.
For sometimes in life's daily round—behind,
Or rather breaking through, the drab routine
Of work and pleasure, comes into the mind
A stillness and a power, a force unseen,
Bearing conviction man is something more
Than thought can demonstrate or eyes have seen.
To hold to this even when the muffled roar
Of distant thunder is no longer heard
Through tinkling of the tinsel bells galore
Is faith.

      If faith too limps, there is a third
Platform for man's take-off to beyond space—
That of the intrepid gambler who averred:
"This life has not so ravishing a face
That when adventure calls I still should cling.
For many causes men have risked her grace—
To climb a mountain or unthrone a king,
For art or science: I for the Supreme.
And if I lose it is a little thing,
But winning I win all. Give me the scheme,
The discipline! Count me with those who try!"

178

Similar but less noble will he seem
Who finds life bitter and, prepared to die,
Takes this last hope of joy worth living by.

SECTION SEVEN

The next demand a wise austerity.
There is a seeming self, an evil ghost,
That covers up your true integrity,
Which to destroy is the last winning post,
Whatever path a man may travel by.
To understand even to the uttermost
But not accomplish this, or even try,
Were like an arctic traveller who sits
In armchair by the fire, and warm and dry,
A rug across his knees, in fancy flits
Through howling blizzard and wild snowy waste.

Not easily the ego-self submits,
But, like guerrilla warfare, if displaced
From one position rises up elsewhere,
And with shrewd strategy he must be faced.

No need for savage measures—better be fair;
Let him have all the body needs, no less—
Also no more. Watch out too for care
What others think of him, vindictiveness,
Grievance or emulation. If there is pride
In learning, deem its damage in excess
Over its value; lay your books aside.
If hope of visions or the healing touch,
Forswear it; if desire to be a guide

To others on the path, know that all such
Are cravings of the ego and abjure.
And do not let the phantom ego clutch
At dream-worlds to surround him and allure
With fancied being, thus to compensate
For life's restrictions and to reassure.

All this is not the path, only the state
From which the prudent wayfarer sets out.
To start without it folly were as great
As try to run up Everest without
Equipment, just in tennis shoes and shirt—
Folly and danger both. Ever about
To turn and turn, build in a sudden spurt,
Demolish in another, forsake your plan
To dance the ego's tune, can cause grave hurt.
The mind, pulled both ways, can betray a man
And leave him far worse off than he began.

SECTION EIGHT

And now the path itself. Many the ways
That men have trod in their eternal quest
For That-which-is. Most suited to our days
A path lived in the world, like others dressed,
Working like others, with no rites or forms.

Turn to look inward and, with mind at rest,
All thought suspended, seek who, what, informs
The living self of you, wherein abides
The pure I-am-ness; probe beyond thought-forms,
Knowing that reason no reply provides;

Nothing for words, only experience;
Not thought but being, being that resides
Rather in heart than head, and issues thence.

Effort is needed. As easy it were to train
A pack of monkeys as the mind. Immense
Persistence. You dispose to calm; again
Thoughts rise insidiously, until once more
The sky is clouded over, and again
You banish, they return. Yet the still core
Of silence can be reached beyond the sound
Of strident thoughts and clamorous uproar.
In silence then, a treasure newly found,
Vibrant awareness rises in the heart,
Like the first crocus daring to break ground
Where lately lay the snow. Brief at the start,
Later spontaneous and pervading all,
Body-sensed, mind-known, and yet from both apart,
Remembrancer, whatever may befall,
More precious than all joys of former days.

Remembrancer, yet powerless to forestall
Resurgent ego; powerless too to raise
That state in you that is not won of right
But may unearned illumine all your ways:
As on some lesser Himalayan height
Facing the mighty Kanchenjunga veiled
In clouds. Sudden the haze parts. Bright
With dazzling whiteness the vast range is hailed
With cries of wonder, while the risen sun
Smites it with reds and golds. Briefly unveiled,
And then the haze drifts back, the splendour done.

Even such a glimpse of the eternal state
Is no assurance that the race is run,
No guarantee a man will not stagnate,
Or that the ego, temporarily dispersed,
Will not return, again to dominate,
A man's last state no better than his first.
Unflagging dedication to the goal
Is needed still, incessant strife to burst
Delusion's bonds, shrewdness to control
The ego's stratagems; not to conceive
Of something to attain, but know the whole
Is now, let but that ego-self take leave
Who seeks to attain, the better to deceive.

Section Nine

Should this way prove too arduous, suppose
The ego-self exists. Such as it is,
And if it is, let it then dispose
Itself to worship, let its litanies
Ascend like incense-smoke about the feet
Of God in Whom the whirling galaxies
And a wild rose, the sum of things complete,
Is a vast harmony to which He said
"Be!" and it is. He Whose Mercy-Seat
Is the incorporeal world about us spread.
Whichever way you turn, behold His Face!
His signs are in the pathways that you tread,
And in the skies; yet in the secret place
Of silence in your heart is His abode.
His power is love. He draws you with His grace,
And with His grace, when needs, as with a goad,
Sharply He thrusts you back from the cliff's edge,

182

Where folly leads or craving, to a road
Shielded from dangers, though with thorns for hedge.

Your constant prayer be that His will be done,
And to submit by your undying pledge;
Yet know that, prayer or no, it will be done,
Being no whim or caprice but the law
Of the Unending and the Unbegun,
The harmony the ancient sages saw
Whereto the heavenly spheres in concord dance,
Which to resist were like a piece of straw
Blown in the wind, but which leads on past trance
To mystic union's unimagined stance.

Section Ten

Some intuition of the butterfly
Impels the caterpillar to undergo
The rigorous chrysalis, gladly to die
To his own state for one he does not know.
How can he know in terms of nibbling leaf?
How dream of flight, being content to grow,
Not live? How will you bring to his belief
Twinkling wings that flit above a flower,
Gay as a lady's wind-inspired kerchief?

What is enjoyment but an ivory tower?
But if life satisfies you, well and good;
Stay on your leaf and nibble. If some power—
Sense of eternity not understood—
Beckons, then follow; never count the cost
(It will cost all). Step forth as a beggar should
To claim a throne, counting his rags well lost;
And never look back, once the threshold crossed.

The Guru

To feel, to know, to be the Christ within—
Can there then be love for Christ on earth,
Walking as man, seen as a man is seen?
Seek not to argue; love has greater worth.
      Love makes man kin

With the Beloved. Such have I known,
Him of the lustrous eyes, Him whose sole look
Pierced to the heart, wherein the seed was sown
Of wisdom deeper than in holy book,
      Of Truth alone

Not to be learned but lived, Truth in its hour
To sprout within the heart's dark wintry earth
And grow a vibrant thing, then, come to power,
To slay the seeming self that gave it birth,
      Or to devour.

Heart of my being, seen outwardly as one
In human form, to draw my human love,
Lord Ramana, Guru, the risen Sun,
Self Manifest, the Guide for all who rove
      Lost and alone

In tangled thoughts and vain imaginings,
Back to pure Being, which Your radiant smile,
Full of compassion for my wanderings,
Tells me always was, though lost this while
      In a world of things.

TO ARUNACHALA

Arunachala!
Thy silence calls me
More powerful than a thousand voices
    O Hill of wonder!

The way is so long, it seemed so near
Whispering shadows, rocks come alive,
Arunachala, Thou calledst me,
    Now free me of fear!

    O Hill of Fire!
Burn my desires to ashes,
But that one desire
    To know.

Shadow-desires
A thousandfold bride,
O Hill of Love!
In thy Grace
    Let me abide.

Sweet flame within my heart
Spread over the universe,
What does it mean?
Hill of Wisdom!
Doubts assail me,
I dare not believe.

Motionless dancing boundless waves
Rose within my mind,

All-engulfing dark waters
On the surface in letters of flame
  " I AM "

         .   .   .   .   .

Like a hawk whose wings
darkened the sky
Thou pouncest on me—a worm in dust—
And carried me off
Into limitless all-knowing radiance.
Lost in freedom-Resplendence-Bliss
Hitherto unknown, undreamt of,
         I found Myself
         . . . .
         I lost Myself.

Beloved! Whither shall I seek thee?
In the abyss of thought,
In the tempest of feeling
I find Thee not.

Plains, rivers, mountains, caves!
         Tell me I pray,
Do you hide Him?
Did He pass your way?
  .   .   .   .   .   .

In vain I spent my days,
In vain I wept at night.
Cool moon and stars!
Lend me your light
To find Him that is hidden
         In my burning heart.

Aruanchala–Bhagavan!
Hill of Water!
Sea of Grace!
Quench my thirst,
Have mercy!

TO BHAGAVAN

A prayer from and inspired by
The Five Hymns to Arunachala—

Like the beating of a heart
One cannot read for tears
Who wrote those words?
Bhagavan—the innermost
   Of oneself.

Immersed in the dark well
Of the dream of life
Greatly am I held
And greatly I strive
   To come out to wake into Light.
But I find it so deep
And forsaken I weep
   Though I know
   It is only a dream.

Unless Thou extend Thy hand of Grace
In mercy, I am lost O Bhagavan!

Immersed in the dark well
Of the dream of life—
How is the lotus of my heart to blossom
Without sight of the sun?
   Thou art the Sun of suns,
   Dispel my darkness,
   Grant me wisdom, I beseech Thee,
So that I may not pine for love of Thee,
In ignorance, O Bhagavan.

Seeking thee within but weakly
I came back, and in sorrow
I pour out my heart. Aid me Bhagavan!

There is naught else but Thee. How is it then
That I alone stand separate from Thee?
   Shake me out of this torpor
   I beseech Thee, Bhagavan.

If spurned by Thee, what rests for me
   But the torment of my dream?
   What hope is left for me?

Could I but gather the suffering of mankind,
Of creation, in my heart, in my hands,
   Their pain my pain—one heart.

There is naught else but Thee.
Who is it that suffers?
   Bhagavan!

I come to knock for release—
It is enough . . . .
      in my dream.

A mother will surely wake her child crying out in sleep
So am I crying out in my cauchemar-dream.
Thou Awakened One, kinder far and nearer than one's
                              own mother,
Is this then Thy all-kindness, Bhagavan,
To leave me thus struggling in deep waters,
—I have lost my moorings—struggling to wake?

Reveal Thyself! Do not continue to deceive and prove me,
    Thou only art Reality!

A prey to my unsteady mind
I lack patience, I lack constancy, I lack purity.

Forgive the grievous wrongs of that poor self,
And do as Thou wilt, Thou who knowest best.
But grant me only ever increasing love
    For Thy Feet.

Thou who art Kindness–Love itself,
Smile with Grace and not with scorn,
On me who knows nothing,
Who comes for refuge to Thee.

BRIEF ETERNITY

Suddenly I was not. Seeing remained,
Not any one who saw. Thoughts still appeared...
No one to think. And all this was not new,
No change of state, for I not only was not
But never had been; only through some spell—
Ignorance—suffering—sin—what name you will*—
Imagined that I was.

    Or just as well
It could be said that suddenly I was,
For Being, Self, whatever name you give,
Just was, and I was That, no other self.

It is a simple thing—no mystery.
The wisdom of the Sages all comes down
To simple being.

    Again this state was lost.
Sisyphus-like, the heavy stone rolled down.
Again was need to tear my love from others,
Alone through the night, with much toil to strive
To the lost homeland, to the Self I am.

Though a world appear, yet will I not cling to it;
Though thoughts arise, yet will I cherish them not.
More deep the mischief of the imposter me
That sees himself and them—or thinks he sees,
He who complains he has not yet achieved.
Who is it that achieves? Or who aspires?
What is there to achieve, when being is
And nothing else beside, no second self?

---

* Ignorance in the Hindu interpretation, suffering in the Buddhist, original sin in the Christian.

The Tiger

All right, let him aspire, the evil ghost—
Better a tiger yoked than a tiger wild.
Let him aspire, but do not be beguiled:
Though he take arms against the rebel host
    Of turbulent desires
        His own lust sires,
    Yet will he never slay
Himself, their leader. All is but a play.

Though he has caught a dim, breeze-wafted strain
Of heavenly music, and from lesser gain
        Turns to the great,
    Yet it is not his fate
    To enter through that gate.
His role in the grand drama is to be
The victim at the altar finally.

The Indweller-II

There is no one here.
Life now is an empty boat
Governed by remote control,
The lunatic helmsman gone.
Waves rise up...
People and things to do...
He, the Invisible, steers.
There is no one else here.

THE INITIATIC DEATH

No other thought my mind can hold:
Night and day on you I cry,
Lord of Mystery manifold,
Death through whom I long to die!

Narrow and dark the passage-way?
Denuded let me enter then;
With both hands will I cast away
All clinging to the world of men.

Like new-wed husband to his bride,
Importunate to you I yearn.
My love, I will not be denied:
How long my pleading will you spurn?

Night and day on you I cry,
All things abandon for your sake.
Now from this dream-life let me die,
At last in Being to awake!

Lord of Mystery manifold,
Grim gateway to Eternal Youth,
Through you alone can man behold
The immortal lineaments of Truth.

Death through whom I long to die,
There is no joy beneath the sky
Were worth a moment's living by
Till you the knot of self untie.
Night and day on you I cry!

THE DARK NIGHT

In the soul's dark night
I knew the taste of tears unshed,
The hopeless seeming fight,
Pain for my daily bread.

The hammer blows of God
Sculptured from the living flesh,
As from a lifeless clod,
The new man made afresh.

The only one escape
Was such my mind could not come by,
Could not even shape—
To curse God and die.

Yet through it all I knew
The mind flagellant and a fake,
Clinging to the untrue.
Self-tortured for desire's sake.

The fake, the evil ghost, the impostor me,
The camel straining at the needle's eye,
Craving and he who craves, must cease to be—
Simply give up and be content to die,
Since there's no other way, better cut quick,
Slay and have done, than make an endless tale,
Flogging then coddling, caring for when sick.
Then sentencing to hunger when he's hale.

Ruthless Compassion! Most compassionate
When most unmoved by anguish of the cry

Of that false self who stands within the gate
That shutters out the radiance of the sky.

Desolation

You bade me lay down my life for your sake, Lord Christ,
   I have laid it here at your feet.
   Is it nothing but a soiled rag
   That you do not deign to accept it,
   That you do not stoop down and raise it?
What now am I to do, despised and rejected of you, Lord Christ?

He who lays down his life for your sake
   Shall find it, you said.
   I have not bargained,
   I have not come as a merchant, Lord Christ,
   I have not asked to find.
   Only I have laid down my life.
What now am I to do, despised and rejected of you, Lord Christ?

You bade me come as your bride, Lord Christ.
   I tore my love from others,
   I came alone through the night,
   With much toil I am here,
   And you have let me stand
   Loveless and unloved before you.
What now am I to do, despised and rejected of you, Lord Christ?

THE LADY OF SHALLOT

Where the mighty river flows
A bleak, grey prison-castle rose
Wherein a lady dwelt, they say,
On whom a lifelong curse there lay:
Not to look out, not to go free,
Only a shadow world to see,
Reflected in a glass.

Daylong a tapestry she wove,
With fantasy but without love.
Thus did the wise ones typify
The life of man, whose days flow by
In a shadow world of mundane things,
Weaving his vain imaginings,
Watching the shadows pass.

Until she saw her love ride by...
Daring to look though she should die,
She rose, cast from her the pretence,
Leapt towards truth, with no defence
But love. The mirror cracked. A shiver
Split the grey walls. The broad river,
Sweeping all things along;

Now bore her on to her true lot
In many-towered Camelot,
To meet the loved one face to face
And, dead to self in mute embrace,
To find the two grown one through love
Beyond all joy for which she strove.
This was the ancient song.

The years flowed down upon the river,
And wisdom and all high endeavour,
Leaving a slum in Camelot.
A poet came and found the plot
And made a pretty tale of it.
Yet still the wisdom and the wit
Of the old sages shines in it.

COMPLETE YOUR WORK!

Bhagavan, was it not you
Who gave these rhymes to me—
My mind the lens they filtered through,
Beautiful to see?

And shall they now stay hid
To lighten no man's way,
A lamp beneath an iron lid,
A prayer with none to pray?

Complete your work, Bhagavan!
Let them shine forth clear,
A light held high for every man,
To guide men to you here.

THE SLEEPING BEAUTY

A pretty children's tale is found
Of how a lady slept spell-bound
Through time's long night, till for her sake
A daring rescuer should break
Through many perils and with a kiss
    Wake her to endless bliss.

In each man's heart she sleeps, her dower
The lost domain of man's true power.
    The same she is
As that coiled serpent of the East
    Who, when released,
Strikes up from stage to higher stage
Till, breaking through the mental cage
Blaze the white-shining ecstasies.

First the wise man gave the knight
The sword of concentration, bright,
Invulnerable; for defence
A cloak, invisible to sense,
Of pure detachment. Yet alone
    The hero fought and won.

Where many fell along the way
To visions, learning, pride, display;
To harlots claiming to be her
Whose waking wakes her rescuer;
Or taverns where the weaklings rest
Called but not chosen for the quest.

Blest now the land!
Humbled the tyrant mind!
Freedom erect to stand
For all mankind!

Now, ever after...
Joy, serene laughter!
Fallen the prison wall
Rooftree and rafter!
Never to be built again
Life's house of pain,
Never hereafter!

Anatta

I was walking along the road when I met
A fool talking fool talk.
"There isn't one, there isn't one! How happy
I am that there isn't one!"
He said, as if it were a song he was singing.
"Isn't one what?" I asked.
"Isn't one me," he said foolishly.
And he walked on looking quite happy.

The Two Windows

Two windows are there: one looks on to space,
The other on the world, both blurred by thought
Of I and mine. This stopped; now not a trace
Through that first window still was seen of ought,
And none to see, no seeker and no sought.
      And yet no blankness this,
      But unimagined bliss,
It's gateway not through terror but through Grace.

"The world and dissolution, day and night,
Both are, eternally." "All things join hands
In cosmic dance," all things now seen aright:
The gnarled and sombre northern pine-trees stand,
And star-shaped jasmine of this sun-baked land;
      Through the breached ego-wall
      Pure love flows out to all,
Even a stray dog draws love as a child might.

Is and Is not, both at once are true,
"Although to sight they seem to alternate."
Life, death, pass over, but they are not you;
Fate fashions life, while you, immaculate,
Remain unchanged beyond life, death and fate.
      You feel love outward flow
      Towards others, while you know
All otherness a dream, the Truth not-two.

To Whom?

Why fumble about blindfold
In the box of things
The future may hold?
They will take to their wings
In whatever form time brings,
Never as told.

Give them no chance
To lodge in your mind,
Or soon you will find
A true devil's dance
Going on without cease,
No respite, no peace.

Let the mind be still,
Like a clear lake
Where no waves break.
Then, come what will,
The thoughts that fly over
Have no cause to hover,
No place to nest
In a mind at rest.

If still they come,
Never follow them home;
Ask only to whom
The thoughts come.

The World

The world's an extension of you—
    Nothing outside.
Let what will betide;
    Only ensue
The inner self of you,
    For this is true.

    For a day you wear
The garb of earth and air,
    Knowledge confined
    To mortal mind:
Only a spell to break,
A dream from which to wake.

    So long it lasts,
Don't think you originate
    The play of fate
    Its shadow casts.
Be a glass polished bright
    To reflect the Light.

But Hui Neng said
    There is no glass.
Let the ego-self be dead,
    This will come to pass.
Then all fate's teeth are drawn
    In that glad dawn.

The World–II

The world's a state you are in;
It's worth is not
Your sad or happy lot,
Whether you lose or win,
But how you shape,
How nearer grow to angel or to ape.

And when its pageant ends?
Why speculate
On the ensuing state?
On you its form depends.
What plant can grow
But from the seeds that in your life you sow?

Rigorous are its laws.
Inexorably
To the last split penny
Effect must follow cause,
So long you hold
Yourself a creature that its clasp can mold.

Till in yourself you know
What self you are:
Nothing to make or mar,
Nothing to change or grow,
From all set free:
The world in you, not you in it to see.

The Shakti

I only know she set my heart aflame
   In youth when tempest tossed;
   In youth, all bearings lost,
Her grace my anchorage, her love my aim.

That was the first; then through the middle years
   Companion on life's ways
Wedded in hopes and not weighed down by fears,
   Solace in sombre days.

And now the third age dawns, the Shakti now,
   Through whom to those who seek
His wisdom flows, His grace confirms the vow
   To assail the sacred peak.

Ergo Non Sum

"I think, therefore I am," Descartes
   Was shrewd enough to say;
Whereby unwittingly he showed the way
   How not to be.
   Let the mind be free
     From every thought,
   Yet conscious still, alert,
    And you will see:
Awareness is—no one to be aware;
Being remains, and yet you are not there.

The Dream-Self

You dreamed you were a postman, say, last night:
And do you ask today if he still is—
The postman-you who never really was
    But only seemed to be?
    It is so plain to see.

What was he then? Had he a self? A soul?
Or was he just a mask you took? And was
The dream with all the dream-folk he found real
    A world no further true
    Than in the mind of you?

Why cling in vain to such a phantom self
Within the brief horizons of a dream?
An intuition of eternity?
    Right—but whose? The dream's?
    What is, or what just seems?

Others-11

If there's I there are others.
The ego-thought makes blind,
The ego-love smothers.
　Turn then the mind
Not to 'I do' but 'doing',
Not to 'I am' but 'being'.
In Consciousness all is; all things join hand
　In cosmic dance,
　All circumstance,
Past and to come, linked in a rhythmic band,
　Is now.
　Things flow as they will flow.
Be then the screen on which the shades are cast,
The Void wherein the rhythmic band flows past;
　Be that eternity
　Wherein moves destiny,
　　Just BE.

THE EXPANSE

That consciousness am I, that Vast Expanse
Of pure serene, that One without a form—
Not even One but Am-ness undefined.
No questions there, no doctrine and no doubt,
Knowledge not known but lived, the clamorous mind
Grown still at last, beyond the stir of time.

From that untroubled state, funnelled below,
Far down, less real, a pseudo-world of forms
Seen or imagined, like a waking dream.

In truth change is not; all in essence IS.
The bubbles on the Ocean do not change
The depths profound. Far off the tinkling notes
Of weal and woe float by upon the breeze,
Heard but not heeded in the Calm supreme
Of Bliss ineffable, pure causeless Bliss
Wherein the worlds have birth. And That I am.

Fantastic Things

Let's say fantastic things,
Let's say that pigs have wings;
But never let us say
This living lump of clay,
This song the Singer sings,
Is author of the play.

The play's an accident,
Nobody wrote it;
It just happened so,
No use to quote it—
So they say.

You just happen to be
Because X met Y;
For awhile you are free
To reason why,
And then you die—
So they say.

But who is that ME in you?
Turn and look steadily.
Who is it that asks who?
Thoughts skip about readily;
Stop them a bit,
Ask who is it
Abides when they quit.
Who are you?

To Christians

You who follow Christ, my advice to you
Is: Put away your clever maps of heaven;
Give up your proofs that only you are right,
All others wrong; stop arguing; turn
To your Christ instead, who did not ask for proofs
But for your life. Give up your life for him,
All your self-will, your I-ness utterly.
He will not compromise, will not accept
Half measures from you. Either he lives or you—
Not both. Step down; make way for him to live
Instead of you; and you will find through him
Obedience follows then to that great word
He laid upon you: to be perfect too,
As God is perfect. Can you not trust in him?

What Remains?

You can't give; you can only refrain from stealing,
Like a servant who says: "All right, I'll let you keep
Your change from marketing, your soap and cheese."
Nothing is yours to give, what 'thing', what 'you'?
You imagine a person, then you think he owns
A cluster of electrons that you call a wife,
A house, a car, children, suits of clothes.
First find out if he exists at all.
In a world where things break down into a cloud
Of whirling atoms with no taste or smell,
No shape or colour, just a grey—what?
Energy? Mass? Not thingness anyway,
And thoughts about it—whirling, never still,
What is it you call 'you'?
This minute's body-shaped bag of atoms?
This minute's thoughts? A you that has the thoughts?
What underlies them? What constant is there,
If anything? You'll not find out by thinking
Because that's thoughts. Nor by arguing.
There's only one way: that's to try and see—
Stop thoughts and see if anything remains.

THE SONG

There isn't one, there isn't one!
How happy I am that there isn't one!
Isn't one what?
Isn't one me.
How happy I am that there isn't one!

If there was one he would be
Mortgaged to age,
A wizened me,
Sickness-ridden years to spend,
Wrung by regret of vanished days,
And in the end,
With choking breath,
Devoured by death.

Free from him who never was,
Free from him and free from care,
Free to work or stand and stare,
Free from fear and from desire,
Incombustible to lust's fierce fire,
Free to tread the cosmic dance,
No longer slave of circumstance!

Beyond our selves and destinies
Only boundless Being is,
And That I am; no other me,
No birth, no death, no destiny.
All that is born shall come to die,
But not the unborn, deathless I.

This Dream

At the gates of my heart
I stand—a beggar
In the howling wind
Clad in rags of thought

Open my love, my King
Open the golden gate
Let Thy splendour stream forth
And flood with light

This shadow-world of sorrow
This face bereft of sight
These shadows of tomorrow
This dream

Mad dogs are at my throat
Shall I perish
A beggar at the gate
Of the King of Grace and Mercy
Is this to be my fate
This dream?

The Poet

I cry the truth of Man
And the thunderous Silence of God
In an old, tired world
Where the poets write about dirt and drains
In poems that sound like prose.

Afraid of joy they are!
Afraid to be glad!
Afraid to shout and sing,
Afraid of youth and love!
They have grown old and grey,
With ditchwater blood and sophisticate minds.

Rise up!
The singing season dawns again
And rhyme makes glad the hearts of men.
Heaven is so close to earth today
You need but twitch a veil away
And all is wonder undefined
In the clear sky of a cloudless mind.

Day and Night

World and dissolution, day and night,
Both are eternally, although to sight
They seem to alternate. Life and death
Are the twin phases of a single breath
Of That-which-is, That which underlies
The self that lives and then reluctant dies,
Not knowing whence or whither. To out-turned gaze
World with its intricate inweaving maze
Of ever-varied forms forever is.
Turn inward and its woven harmonies
Are gone with him that saw them. Nought remains
That eye can see or thought, though it contains
All things, can comprehend. Only the Void
Unknowable whereon the worlds float past
Like foam-flakes on the Ocean. How shall mind
Pierce to what was before it, or how find
The womb that gave it birth? No aggregate
Of thoughts and feelings, no conglomerate
Of forms, endures; and yet, though figments pass,
"Life like a dome of many-coloured glass
Stains the white radiance of eternity,"*
And all things are and are not endlessly.

---

* Shelly, *Adonais*

The Waning Moon

Oh never think the moon compulsive wanes:
Fate is compulsion only to the fool
Who flees eternity to seek time's gains
And, frog-like, finds his ocean in a pool.

Man and the moon have choice, yet it is not
Whether to go or stay; immutable
Their path and phases of their path; their lot
Written in light, most ineluctable.

Their choice is whether, clinging to their place,
To stumble on, flogged by fate's iron whip,
Or, as the bride flees to her lord's embrace,
Set sail with love for breeze and faith for ship.

The Elixir of Youth

The frosty years have in their grip
This ailing body that at last
Into Death's refuse-bin must slip.
    Then let it go,
      Quick be it or slow,
Like autumn flower in wintry blast.

For I have drunk youth's elixir,
His joy made firm, his follies fled.
Life like a May-day chorister
    Throbs into song.
    The heart, grown strong,
Dances and sings where grief lies dead.

This world and body are not me.
They are a dream from which to wake.
Whatever in their fate may be
    Cannot destroy
    The vibrant joy
Or turn to night the bright daybreak.

When even imperfect sight can bring
Such joyful certitude as this,
Who to the seeming self would cling,
In a barren land where no birds sing,
Lost to Awareness, Being, Bliss?

OTHERNESS

Save me, O Lord, from otherness! And yet
There is no other nor no me to save;
Thou only art, in countless forms declared;
Thou wert and nothing else before the worlds,
And Thou art now as then.
All change and pass, only Thy Face endures.
What then is man? Other he cannot be:
There is no other. He who is One, Alone,
Unchangeably, illimitably IS,
Yet, without ceasing from His Changelessness,
Speaks all the tale of laws and flowing lives,
All seeming strife within the womb of Peace.
Thou art His spoken word; yet listen well
And all the universe is spoken through thee;
Thou art the lens through which the rays divine
Pass to spread out in this wide pageantry.
Give up thy self and no self can remain
But That which IS; if thou give up or not
Yet at the end must all return to Him
As dream-forms melt in waking; at the end
He IS and otherness has never been
And all thy strife was needless and the course
Of that which thou calledst thee is before time
And but unrolled as pictures on a screen.
Why wilt thou cling to that which never was?
What refuge is there from the Eternal Now,
The Truth that changes not? In ignorance awhile
A seeming self a seeming refuge finds
From peace in strife, from bliss in famished quest

Of joys still fleeting, in frustrated life
That mocks and swings its still ungathered fruit
Just beyond reach and then, receding far,
Leaves hunger and a memoried regret,
And the few gathered fruits taste sour at last
And all ungathered, fair yet far, still mock
With might-have-been. Yet all that hides
    Truth's Self
And lures, delusive-fair, then breaks and mocks,
Leaving the embittered traveller unappeased
Like one who sought relief in a mirage
And finds the pitiless sun and the wide sand,
All that disguises Truth's white radiance
Under prismatic myriad-gleaming points,
Gleaming and ending, flashing from the dark,
In phantom forms, then melting into dark,
Dreams insubstantial, form ephemeral,
All is the Face of Truth for who can see,
All is the Word blown forth in waves of song,
All threads in thy life's tapestry declare
The Truth behind Thee. Men shall not escape
From That which is to that which fancy builds,
Frail as the builder.
Listen! In all things is the Voice of God.
Turn where ye will, there is the Face of God.

The Wind

I am a pipe the wind blows through,
Be still, it is the wind that sings.
The course of my life and the things that I do
And the seeming false and the seeming true
Are the tune of the wind that neither knows
Good and ill, nor joys and woes.
But the ultimate awe is deeper yet
Than song or pipe or storm;
For pipe and tune are the formless wind
That seemed for a while to take form.
And words are good to escape from words
And strife to escape from strife,
But silence drinks in all the waves
Of song and death and life.

63
78 - Juipter + Saturn
82 exoteric Shell
118 . Karma